# SINGING SOLDIERS

"This is exactly the music I want the troops to hear."

*Lincoln*

"Without music we couldn't have any army."

*Lee*

*Other books by*
*Paul Glass and Louis C. Singer:*


SONGS OF FOREST AND RIVER FOLK
SONGS OF HILL AND MOUNTAIN FOLK
SONGS OF THE SEA
SONGS OF THE WEST
SONGS OF TOWN AND CITY FOLK

# A History of the Civil War in Song

# SINGING SOLDIERS

## (THE SPIRIT OF THE SIXTIES)

Selections and historical commentary
**PAUL GLASS**
BROOKLYN COLLEGE of the
CITY UNIVERSITY of NEW YORK

Musical arrangements for piano and guitar
**LOUIS C. SINGER**

Foreword by **JOHN HOPE FRANKLIN**

**A DA CAPO PAPERBACK**

Library of Congress Cataloging in Publication Data

Glass, Paul, comp.
   Singing soldiers = The spirit of the sixties.

   (A Da Capo paperback)
   1964 ed. published under title: The spirit of the
sixties.
   For voice and piano and/or guitar.
   Reprint of the ed. published by Grosset & Dunlap,
New York.
   Bibliography: p.
   1. 1. United States—History—Civil War, 1861-1865—
Songs and music. I. Singer, Lou, 1912-      arr.
II. Title.
[M1637.G6S7 1975]            784.7′19′73            75-14-127
ISBN 0-306-80021-7

First paperback printing 1975
Second paperback printing 1988
ISBN 0-306-80021-7


This Da Capo Press paperback edition of *Singing Soldiers* is
an unabridged republication of the 1968 edition
published in New York. The book was originally
published under the title of *The Spirit of the Sixties* in 1964.


Copyright © 1964 by Paul Glass and Louis C. Singer.
Copyright © 1968 by Paul Glass and The Estate of Louis C. Singer.


Published with the permission of Paul Glass


Published by Da Capo Press, Inc.
A subsidiary of Plenum Publishing Corporation
233 Spring Street, New york, N.Y. 10013

# Foreword

There were so many unique features of the Civil War that one is tempted to conclude that few if any events in the history of the United States have been so replete with the unusual, the remarkable, and even the bizarre. On the field of battle, brothers were fighting brothers and slaves were fighting their masters. Behind the lines, white laborers were rioting against black workers and gentlewomen were smuggling and spying. Each year witnessed a progression toward the unbelievable, until finally the Confederacy began enlisting Negroes to fight for the preservation of slavery and states' rights.

In this great epic nothing was more remarkable than the emergence of a great literature of music and song on both sides of the line. Masters and slaves, soldiers and sailors, Republicans and Democrats, mothers and fathers, sons and daughters were among those whose songs gave expression to their innermost feelings. Even in the midst of battle, when feelings were running high and dangers were imminent, Confederate soldiers serenaded Union soldiers and vice versa. Out of these efforts, ranging from the most casual improvisations to the most carefully constructed compositions, came a wealth of song that has become a most important heritage of the Civil War.

There have been many collections of Civil War songs, some more satisfactory than others. In this collection, Paul Glass has displayed not only remarkable knowledge of Civil War musical literature but a keen understanding of the social and political—and military—events behind the music. The piano settings by Louis Singer are not only fitting but they greatly enhance the value of the work. The result is a massive and masterful achievement; and all who are interested in this period are deeply indebted to them for their efforts.

JOHN HOPE FRANKLIN

# Acknowledgments

Grateful acknowledgment is hereby made to Joseph V. Glass, my son, for his valuable research assistance. I am very thankful to Fred Blum of the Library of Congress; to Philip Miller, Sirvart Poladian and Karl Kroeger of the Music Division of the New York Public Library for their generous efforts and assistance in making available important material; to Mrs. Gladys Graves of the Brooklyn Public Library for her assistance with select pieces of "musical prints" of the period; and to my wife Evelyn for editorial assistance.

I am indebted to Bobbs Merrill Co. for permission to quote from "The Blue and The Gray" by Henry S. Commager; and from "The Life of Billy Yank and Johnny Reb" by Bell Irwin Wiley; to Houghton Mifflin Co., to quote from "A Diary From Dixie," ed. by Ben Ames Williams; to Doubleday & Co., Inc. to quote from "Folk Songs of North America" by Alan Lomax; to Harcourt Brace & World, Inc. to quote from "Storm Over The Land" by Carl Sandburg; to Cooper Square Publishing Co. for permission to use many of the illustrations; to Golden Press, Inc. and the Ridge Press, Inc. for permission to use the illustrations from "The American Civil War" by Earl Schenck Miers, (c) 1961.

PAUL GLASS

# Contents

## PART ONE

### *Patriotism*

### *Politics*

## PART TWO

## PART THREE

## PART FOUR

### Somebody's Darling

## PART FIVE

### Memories

# The Piano Settings

The format of popular sheet music of the "sixties" consisted of a vocal line on one staff and an accompaniment of chords in a rhythmic pattern on two staves. Such a design was quite suitable for the performance practices of the period, especially for the soloist performing in concert style. Contemporary usage, however, where the home and the classroom are sources of music making, required consideration and some modification of the format while at the same time preserving the stylistic flavor of the music of the period.

We decided on a present day practical technique where the vocal line is also placed into the piano part. This enhances the edition and extends its usefulness. The average player will find that the song becomes more meaningful and enjoyable. For the classroom teacher this format will become an effective means in leading group singing.

The melodic and harmonic character of the songs have been faithfully preserved. Where I did alter a harmony or voice leading, it was for the betterment of the edition. Occasionally, I have transposed songs to suitable keys for practical purposes of performance. The chord symbols above the vocal line will enable a guitar or banjo to partake of the accompaniment.

These piano settings are neither simplifications nor ornamentations. Their purpose is to bring into sharp focus the character and style of our musical heritage. With this continuity throughout the entire collection, a variety of musical ensembles can partake and enjoy the grandeur of the period and reflect upon our traditions.

LOUIS C. SINGER

# Introduction

The songs and hymns that Billy Yank and Johnny Reb sang in camp, on the march and in battle, and the ones their folks sang at home stemmed from the same roots of American music. Though the shot fired at Fort Sumter on that fateful morning of April 12, 1861 cut the nation in half, music gave the North and the South a spiritual oneness. For the melodies of the "sixties" reveal an accretion of more than two hundred years of America's colorful musical history and experience. It was during this period that a distinctive melodic style emerged, with a national flavor. Evangelical in character, these melodies were a unique amalgam of Negro and White Spirituals, Gospel tunes, Minstrel Songs, foreign folk songs, and Stephen Collins Foster melodies. The flavor of the "sixties" flowered from a little Psalter that Henry Ainsworth prepared for the Pilgrims, and which Henry Wadsworth Longfellow described in "The Courtship of Miles Standish," from the "Instruction Books" for better singing of the Psalms by John Tufts and Thomas Walther written in 1721, from those "Singing Schools" and itinerant music teachers whom James Fenimore Cooper portrays so vividly in "The Last Of The Mohicans," and lastly from those revival folk hymns and "shape note" hymnals with their choral settings which embody the core of the American muse.

Slowly through the years these tunes and chants journeyed up the river and caught the ears of song writers, who were the forerunners of Tin Pan Alley. When the "fifties" rolled around, the Minstrel Show, the Topical Song, the Singing Family troupes, and Stephen Foster melodies were in their heyday. "Swanee River" was on everybody's tongue. Dwight's *Journal of Music* reports in 1852:

> Pianos and guitars groan it, night and day; sentimental young ladies sing it; sentimental young gentlemen warble it in midnight serenades; all bands play it; the milkman mixes it up with the harsh ding-dong accompaniment of his tireless bell.

and in far off Vipurii, Finland, American girls were requested to sing that "beautiful American song, 'Swanee River.'"

## The Songs

The decade of the Civil War was ripe and ready for that new flavor, long confined, which burst forth and fused words with new moving strains of melody. Never before in history was there such an outpouring of popular patriotic music, written with such vivid descriptiveness and reflecting the spirit of the time. The unusual mixture of sentiments was well expressed in one of Stephen Foster's most interesting compositions, "The Song of All Songs," copyrighted in 1863. For the chorus of this song Foster wrote:

> "Old songs! New songs! Ev-ry kind of song,
> I noted them down as I read them along."

He then set the titles into a rhyming pattern and created his own song—"The Song of All Songs." Here are a few verses which combine the different topics of the period: (Some of these songs will be found in this collection.)

> 2.
> There was "Abraham's Daughter" "Going out upon a spree,"
> With "Old Uncle Snow" "In the Cottage by the sea."
> "If your foot is pretty, show it" "At Lanigan's ball;"
> And "Why did she leave him" "On the raging Canawl?"
> "I don't think much of you" "We were boys and girls together."

"Do they think of me at home?" "I'll be free and easy still"
"Give us now a good Commander" with "The Sword of Bunker-Hill."

*Chorus:*    Old Songs, etc.

### 3.

"When this Cruel War is over," "No Irish need apply,"
"For, every thing is lovely," and the "Goose hangs high."
"The Young Gal from New-Jersey," "Oh! wilt thou be my bride?"
And "Oft in the Stilly Night" "We'll all take a ride."
"Let me kiss him for his Mother" "He's a Gay Young Gambolier;"
"I'm going to fight mit Sigel" and "De bully Lager-bier."
"Hunkey Boy is Yankee Doodle," "When the Cannons loudly roar."
"We are coming, Father Abraham, six hundred thousand more!"

*Chorus:*    Old Songs, etc.

### 4.

"In the days when I was hard up" with "My Mary Ann,"
"My Johnny was a Shoemaker," "Or Any other Man!"
"The Captain with his whiskers" and "Annie of the Vale,"
Along with "Old Bob Ridley," "A riding on a Rail!"
"Rock me to sleep, Mother," "Going round the Horn;"
"I'm not myself at all," "I'm a Bachelor forlorn."
"Mother, is the Battle over?" "What are the men about?"
"How are you, Horace Greely?" "Does your Mother know you're out?"

*Chorus:*    Old Songs, etc.

### 5.

"We won't go home till morning," with "The Bold Privateer"
"Annie Lisle" and "Zouave Johnny" "Riding in a Rail-road Kerr;"
"We are coming, Sister Mary," with "The Folks that put on airs."
"We are marching along" with "The Four-and-Thirty Stars."
"On the other side of Jordan" "Don't fly your Kite too high!"
"Jenny's coming o'er the Green" to "Root, Hog or die!"
"Our Union's Starry Banner," "The Flag of Washington,"
Shall float victorious o'er the land, from Maine to Oregon!

*Chorus:*    Old Songs, etc.

During the years of the intense conflict, North and South borrowed songs from each other and used them for the cause of freedom as each saw it at the time. Valid copyrights of each other were tossed to the winds. Parody, satire and variation were fruitful devices, frequently employed by both sides. Abraham Lincoln and Jefferson Davis each received his share of ribbing. In the early stages of the war and during McClellan's indecision on the Potomac, the South chanted "Where Are You Going Abe Lincoln?" to the tune of "Lord Lovel."

Abe Lincoln he stood at the White House gate,
    Combing his milk-white steed,
Along came his lady, Lizzie Todd,
    A wishing her lover good speed, speed, speed,
    A wishing her lover good speed.

"And where are you going, Abe Lincoln?" she said,
    "And where are you going," said she;
"I am going, my dear lady Lizzie Todd,
    Old Richmond for to see, see, see,
    Old Richmond for to see."

"And when will you be back, Abe Lincoln," she said,
    "And when'll you be back," said she,

"In sixty or ninety days, at most,
　　I'll return to you, fair Lizzie, zie, zie,
　　I'll return to you, fair Lizzie."

The North responded in 1861 with a rhyme to the lively tune of "Old Dan Tucker."

With stars and stripes and martial glee,
We'll send Jeff Davis up a tree;
His traitorous band must follow suit,
Because they like that kind of fruit.

Get out of the way old Jeff Davis
Out the way old Jeff Davis
Out the way old Jeff Davis
You're too late to come to enslave us.

In a song "The Abe-iad" the South attempted to disparage Lincoln's growing popularity with the cause of "Union and Abolition."

Abe Lincoln was a citizen of very small renown,
A railing abolitioner of little Springfield town;
Abe's party said: November comes, don't let us fail,
To meet the other parties all, and beat them with a rail.

And when "Ole Secesh" got mad the rhymes became mighty rough:

With a beard that was filthy and red,
His mouth with tobacco bespread,
Abe Lincoln sat in the gay White House
A-wishing that he was dead.

The North shot back with a fearful "razzle-dazzle" in a song "Jeff Davis' Dream."

Jeff Davis awoke one morn' from a dream
A horrible dream, a horrible dream.
He jumped from his bed with a terrible scream,
A terrible scream he gave.

He dreamed that a mudsill stood close to his bed,
In a garb of a Zouave in flannel and red,
With a noose made of hemp slipping over his head,
Saying, "Come along traitor with me."

# The South—Dixie

"Dixie" was one of the most parodied songs of the war. One of the most successful verses was composed by General Albert Pike of Arkansas. He was Indian commissioner to the Confederate government and, curiously, a native of Vermont.

Southrons, hear your country call you!
Up! lest worse than death befall you!
To arms! to arms! to arms! in Dixie!

Lo, all the beacon fires are lighted,
Let all hearts be now united!
To arms! to arms! to arms! in Dixie!

*Chorus:*
Advance the flag of Dixie! Hurrah! Hurrah!
For Dixie's land we'll take our stand,
To live or die for Dixie.

Another Southern version titled "Dixie War Song" rhymed:

> Hear ye not the sounds of battle,
> Sabres clash and muskrats rattle?
> To arms! to arms! to arms! in Dixie!

"Dixie" was originally composed by a Northern song writer, Dan Decatur Emmett, in 1859 and the South adopted it as their rallying song. The North could not resist its catchy quality and effectiveness, and the Wolverines from Michigan brought out their own verses, showing a concern for the Stars and Stripes:

> Away down South where grows the cotton,
> Seventy-six seems quite forgotten!
> Far away, far away, far away, Dixie land.
> And men with rebel shout and thunder
> Tear our good old flag asunder
> Far away, far away, far away, Dixie land.

And from an Illinois soldier on the famous "mud march" after the battle at Fredericksburg, came a chant to the tune of "Dixie:"

> "I wish I was in St. Law County
> Two years up and I had my bounty
> Away, look away, away, away."*

This version was composed by "The Bucket-eers" who were members of Ward's Legion in Texas and titled "Rum Raid at Velasco."

> One night when we were getting dry,
> A little old Whiskey was the cry;
> Away, away, away, down South in Texas;
>
> The boys hit up they had a plan,
> To rob the commissary man,
> Away, away, away, down South in Texas.
>
> *Chorus:*
>   O, when we get the whiskey, away, away,
>   We'll drink old rum, and think we're some,
>   Away down South in Texas.
>
> We bored the floor through and through,
> And it was then the whiskey flew,
> Away down South in Texas.

# The North—Battle Hymn of the Republic

It is a curious coincidence of history and a glowing testament to the spiritual oneness of music that the melody that pulsed the lines of Julia Ward Howe's poem came from the South. The tune is ascribed to William Steffe, a Southern composer of popular Sunday School songs dating from as early as 1856. Whatever the origin of the tune may be, the impact of this song was so powerful that Theodore Roosevelt, writing in 1908 to Joel Chandler Harris—then president of the Uncle Remus Society—expressed the thought:

> "that sooner or later all Americans would grow to realize that in this Battle Hymn of
> the Republic we had what really ought to be a great National treasure, something that
> all Americans would grow to know intimately—"

The tune was a favorite with John Brown who was hanged on December 2, 1859 and was sung
*Wiley, B. I., *The Life of Billy Yank*, p. 162.

at his funeral. A little more than a year later, the shot at Fort Sumter rang throughout the states, and the new song, "John Brown's Body," sprang into being.

Colonial Fletcher Webster's Twelfth Massachusetts Regiment was the first to adopt it as a marching song. By 1862, thousands of soldiers were marching off to fight with the "Battle Hymn of the Republic" on their lips.

While visiting Washington during the first year of the war, Julia Ward Howe received an indelible impression of the commotion and tumult, and in one evening the immortal poem was born. She writes in her "Reminiscences:"

> "That night I lay in the dark room, line after line shaping itself in my mind, and verse after verse. I sprang out of bed and groped about in the dim twilight to find a bit of paper and the stump of a pen which I remembered to have had the evening before. On the occasion now spoken of, I completed my writing, went back to bed and fell fast asleep."

She also wrote: "My poem did some service in the Civil War. I wish very much that it may do good service in the peace, which, I pray God may never be broken."

# The Wagon

The song "Wait for the Wagon" was at the height of its popularity during the war years. It was composed by R. B. Buckley in the "fifties." He was the originator of that Minstrel troupe known as the "Buckley serenaders." Both sides used it for lampoons and propaganda. "The Union Wagon" couldn't be split:

> "There's none can smash the wagon, 'tis patented and strong,
> And built of pure devotion, by those who hate the wrong;
> Its wheels are made of freedom, which patriots adore,
> The spokes when rightly counted, just number forty-four."
>
> *Chorus:*
> Keep in the wagon,
> The Old Union Wagon
> The oft-tested wagon,
> While millions take a ride.

"The Southern Wagon" was "Respectfully dedicated and hitched up for the President, officers and men of the Confederate Army" and was written when only seven states were "on the wagon."

> Secession is our watchword, our rights we will demand;
> To defend our homes and firesides we pledge our hearts and hand.
> Jeff Davis is our President, with Stephen by our side;
> Brave Beauregard, our General, will join us in our ride.
>
> *Chorus:*
> Oh, wait for the wagon.
> The Dissolution wagon;
> The South is our wagon,
> And we'll all take a ride.
>
> Our wagon is the very best, the running gear is good;
> Stuffed 'round the sides with cotton and made of Southern wood;
> Carolina is the driver, with Georgia by her side;
> Virginia holds the flag up while we'll all take a ride.
>
> There was Tennessee and Texas also in the ring;
> They wouldn't have a government where cotton wasn't king,
> Alabama and Florida have long ago replied;
> Mississippi and Louisiana are anxious for the ride.

The North sallied that the "Union Wagon" was built of sturdier stuff:

> "The makers of our wagon were men of solid wit,
> They made it out of charter oak that would not be split.
> Its wheels are of materials, the strongest and the best;
> And two are named the North and South, and two the East and West."

The progress of secession was itemized in "The Southern Wagon" by Will Shakespeare Hays, writing under the pen name of Jerry Blossom. He was a prolific song writer from Kentucky and noted for that successful and moving song "The Drummer Boy of Shiloh." Here are a few verses from Hays' "The Southern Wagon."

> "Jeff Davis built a wagon and on it put his name
> And Beauregard was driver of secession's ugly frame.
> The horse he would get hungry as most horses do
> They had to keep the collar tight to keep from pulling through.
>
> The axles wanted greasing, the body was not wide.
> North Carolina jumped into it, Mississippi by her side;
> Virginia took a cushioned seat and Lou'siana next,
> South Carolina got to scrouging and Florida got vexed.
>
> They asked Kentucky to take a ride, she said the horse was blind;
> She shook her head at seeing Tennessee jump on behind.
> But Jeff assured her all was right, the wagon it was new.
> Missouri winked at Beauregard and said it would not do."

# The Spirit

The most eloquent tribute to the spirit of "oneness" and the forcefulness of music is revealed in those touching episodes when Billy Yank and Johnny Reb exchanged songs and played for each other at outposts along the "Rapahannock" and "Chatahoochee" Rivers, and other sectors of the front.

> ". . . At Fredericksburg, during the war's second winter . . . a crack group of Union musicians posted on the Northern bank of the Rapahannock staged a concert unique in the annals of war. The program began with a medley of Northern airs—patriotic tunes and war songs.
>
> " 'Now give us one of ours,' shouted the Confederate across the river. Without hesitation the band swung into the tunes of 'Dixie,' 'My Maryland,' and 'The Bonnie Blue Flag.' "*

At Murfreesboro, on the night before the great battle, Federal and Confederate troops exchanged favorite songs. An element of competition was introduced into these informal concerts. After a Confederate band would run through a tune, the Union band would attempt a better rendition.

> "In January 1863 . . . Lieutenant W. J. Kincheloe of the Forty-ninth Virginia regiment wrote to his father: 'We are on one side of the Rapahannock, the Enemy on the other. . . . Our boys will sing a Southern song, the Yankees will reply by singing the same tune to Yankee words.' "*

Thus for brief moments the animosities of war were lost in nostalgic reveries and as the strains of an old favorite faded away, tears could be found on the cheeks of old veterans who on the morrow were to walk unflinchingly into the maelstrom of battle.

Music was a favorite recreation of both armies. Many soldiers on leaving home for the war took violins, guitars, flutes and other musical instruments with them and entertained their comrades at camp with informal concerts. Singing helped the troops to combat fatigue and weari-

*Wiley, B. I., *The Life of Johnny Reb*, pp. 317–18.

ness on the march, to relieve boredom and homesickness, and to give courage in battle. The desire to sing was so strong that soldiers on outpost duty had to be reprimanded for lifting their voices and giving away their positions.

Chanting some piece of doggerel helped pass the time and keep the spirits going. Here is an adaptation to mess call:

> Soupy, soupy, soupy, without any bean,
> Porky, porky, porky, without any lean,
> Coffee, coffee, coffee, without any cream.°

And this one could come from around the poker table:

> The king will take the queen,
> And the queen will take the jack.
> And down we march to Dixie's land,
> With knapsacks on our back.

Gripes about rations were prevalent with both armies. This one was sung to the tune of "America."

> My rations are S. B.
> Taken from porkers three
> Thousand years old.
> And hardtack cut and dried,
> Long before Noah died—
> From what was left aside,
> Ne'er can be told.°°

## The Songsters

When the boys in "The Blue" and those in "The Gray" took up arms, popular and patriotic songs streamed from the pens of American song writers. In the North, major contributions came from such well known composers as George F. Root, Henry C. Work, Charles Carroll Sawyer and the ballad singer, Walter Kittredge. From the South, John Hill Hewitt, Harry MacCarthy, St. George Tucker, Will Shakespeare Hays, A. C. Blackmarr and Hermann Schreiner vied with scores of unknown bards in composing songs for the war effort. In response to the enormous demands of the soldiers and the folks at home, publishers in New York, Philadelphia, Chicago, Richmond, and New Orleans, ground out thousands of songs on broadsides, on folding cards and in pocket songbooks. With a good soldier's market, publishers on both sides produced hundreds of titles for the *Pocket Songster*. Some of the names that adorned the Northern booklets were: *The Camp Fire Songster, Tony Pastor's Union Songster, The Little Mac Songster,* produced during McClellan's heyday, *The Frisky Irish Songster, Nat Austin's New Comic and Sentimental Song Book, Bugle Call,* compiled by the prolific song writer George F. Root, and *Beadle's Union Dime Song Book.* The list from the South was equally impressive with such titles as: *Songs of the South, Beauregard Songster, Stonewall Song Book, Songs of Love and Liberty, General Lee Songster,* the *Southern Flag Song Book,* and *Rebel Rhymes and Rhapsodies.* Both sides were well supplied and stocked with songs.

The *Pocket Songster* was an active reporter of events and left a colorful chronicle of history. In the song *Rising of the North,* actual names of families were given to commemorate those who gave their sons as soldiers:

> New Hampshire sends six Sanborn boys;
> With them Brown Barkers seven,
> The Twolby's brave, the sons and dads;
> Of six and five, make eleven.

°Wiley, B. I., *The Life of Billy Yank,* pp. 157 & 163.
°°Dolpf, Edward, *Sound Off,* p. 314.

The song continues with the Kays'—Cookes'—Butwells' and with the state of Minnesota, Connecticut, Vermont, New York, Ohio, and Pennsylvania.

Here is a jibe at "English Neutrality."

> We're building ships now for the Empire of China,
>     Says the old innocent raising her eyes;
> But we know very well, they're for Jeff and his Dinah,
>     So what's the use of telling such lies.

And the German soldier laments in "Corporal Schnapps."

> Mine heart ish broken into little pits,
> I tell you friend what for;
> Mine schweetheart, von coot patriotic girl,
> She trives me off mit der war.

The events at Bull Run are recounted in "Gwine to Run all Night," to Foster's song, "De Camptown Races:"

> At Bull Run dere I got too near, doo-dah! doo-day!
> I came away with a flee in my ear, doo-day! doo-dah-day!
>
> Ole Zollicoffer came on de track, doo-day! doo-day!
> De bob tail jay him on his back, . . . etc., etc.

"Mickey O'Flaherty's off for a Soldier" sang of his fight for the "Flag of the Faithful and Free." And the perplexed "eligible" makes some plans in "Come in out of the Draft, or How Are You, Conscript?"

> I soon made up my mind that I would take a wife,
> For she could save my cash, and I could save my life.

The *Pocket Songster* recounted "General Lee at the Battle of the Wilderness," "The Bombardment of Vicksburg," "Ladies to the Hospital," "The Zouave Boys," and many other aspects of the war and human sentiment.

# The Burdens

Many of the soldiers on both sides were young boys, away from home for the first time. They were too young to dream of "Lorena" or "Aura Lea," but not too old to yearn for "Mother." George Frederick Root's "Just Before the Battle, Mother" expresses these emotions. A letter from a soldier in a New York regiment is printed on the title page of Charles Sawyer's song, "Mother Would Comfort Me." The title is taken from the last line of the soldier's letter. "Weeping Sad and Lonely" was so mournful that many officers forbade its singing. These are typical of other titles in the collection.

As the war entered its third year many of the songs began to reflect the sentiments of a people weary of civil strife but determined to win. "When This Cruel War Is Over" was answered by the Confederates with "When upon the Field of Battle."

"Lorena" was the most popular love ballad of the Confederate soldiers. It brought forth memories of the past and hopes of an early reunion with the loved "lassies" back home. "Aura Lea" was the counterpart for the Northern armies. This song has retained its popularity and is a "song hit" today.

Memories of the war are recalled in such songs as "We've Drunk from the Same Canteen" and "We Were Comrades Together in the Days of War." The emotions of the soldiers linger poignantly in these lyrics and melodies.

> We've shared our blankets and tent together,
> And marched and fought in all kinds of weather.
> And hungry and full we've been;

Had days of battle and days of rest;
But this memory I cling to and love the best—
We have drunk from the same canteen.

Patriotic songs stirred and agitated the American people for a generation. Harry MacCarthy, noted comedian and entertainer, gave the South "The Bonnie Blue Flag" and the North responded with "The Bonnie Blue Flag with the Stripes and Stars" written by Colonel J. L. Geddes of the Eighth Iowa Infantry. He composed it while a prisoner of war at Selma, Alabama. George F. Root's "Battle Cry of Freedom" was answered by Hermann L. Schreiner, a prolific Southern song writer. James Ryder Randall wrote "Maryland, My Maryland" and Septimus Winner gave the North a "My Maryland." The entertainer and musical groups like the Hutchinsons popularized the songs of the period. But Tony Pastor, that noted comedian, did more than sing and contribute songs. He left to posterity a piece of rhetoric which is so indigenous to the American style, that I am compelled to put it into this introduction. Before addressing his audience he sang, "The Union Volunteer" and then began with:

> Feller sovereigns of the great glorious, victorious and notorious E Pluribus Unum of the 33 States, seven territories and one District including New Jersey, Central Park and Staten Island. I stand here upon the live oak platform of eternal Union, and I appeal to every man and woman on this side of Hell-Gate of Secession and every fire eater t'other side of Jordan and I ask: Is this growing and conglomerated and confederated plantation of the planets of liberty, concentrated and cemented by the blood and sweat of patriotic heroes—bounded on the east by Daybreak, on the west by Eternity Peak, or the north by the Aurora Borealis, on the south by Eternal Sunshine, sugar chivalry, white cotton, black wool, yaller fever, and secession . . . . to be split asunder because a rail splitter happens to be voted into the old arm chair of Washington? No. Forbid it, ye mouldering bones of Revolutionary heroes, war-horses and pitchforks, whose every battlefield is holy ground—from the blood baptized plains of Lexington to Long Island, from Bunker Hill to Trenton where Washington and Knox gave the foe a Christmas box.
>
> They talk of dividing the Union by the rule of short division; but when they come to cipher it out, and prove it, where will they find paper enough to hold the figures? Why, they'd be like the stars in the great Celestial Union above us, the more they try to 'numerate 'em the more they couldn't count 'em. How would they divide the flag that has floated in triumph from the Halls of Montezuma to the North Pole and Grinnal's land. Why, if they should divide the flag, give the stars to the Unionists and the stripes to the backs of the Seceders, who would alter our national motto of E Pluribus Unum into E Blunderbus Shoot 'em. How shall we divide our national currency? Give the heads to the North and the tails to the South, if they dare to 'run the hazard of the die.' Why let the true-blues man the guns (imitating shooting) and give the bullets to the rebels, while the American eagle standing on the Rocky Mountain, with the Stars and Stripes in one claw and with his thumb in his nose shall cry: Set up the pins—you can't come it—singing, Air, Dixie.

> Sugar cane and cotton bail
> To split the Union's bound to fail
> Huzza—Huzza.

# The Impact

The "sixties" gave rise to a distinctive melodic style and the impact of it is still with us today. Who does not know "Tenting Tonight," "Tramp, Tramp, Tramp," "Dixie," "The Battle Cry of Freedom," and the songs of today—"Aura Lea," (Love Me Tender), "The Yellow Rose of Texas," and the immortal "Battle Hymn of the Republic."

In 1866 William Gilmore Simms wrote:

> "The emotional literature of a people is as necessary to the philosophical historian as are the mere details of events in the progress of a nation. . . . It shows with what spirit the popular mind regarded the course of events. In poetry and song the emotional

nature is apt to declare itself without reserve—speaking out with a passion which dis-
dains subterfuge, through media of imagination and fancy which glows and weeps
with emotions that gush freely and freshly from the heart. With this persuasion, we can
also forgive the muse who, in her fervor, is sometimes forgetful of her art."*

The songs in this collection have been selected from a rich treasure of human experience and artistic effort. Many hundreds of songs in "Pocket Songsters" and individual pieces of sheet music were examined. It was also necessary to look into Army journals, state histories, historical records and diaries. The problems of publication made the omission of many worthy songs a painful duty. The bases for selection were: (a) the most singable and stylistically appealing melodies; (b) the songs that portray the sentiments and feelings of the soldiers and the people at home; (c) historical interest; (d) the songs which may have lasting appeal.

With flight and fancy of imagination, the humble poet and musician has recorded the spirit of a people. Though some of the events of the period divided them, in the union of words and music they achieved a oneness. Herein lies the sincerity which makes these songs epochal.

*Simms, W. G., War Poetry of the South.

# Part One

# *Patriotism*
# *Politics*
# *Portraits*

# *Patriotism*

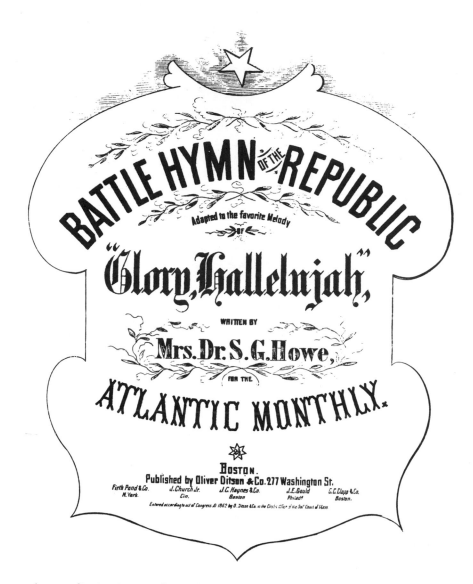

This song has a distinctive quality of its own. When the famed leader and friend of Lincoln's, Colonel Elmer E. Ellsworth, was killed while taking down a Rebel flag in Alexandria, Virginia, his troops sang:

> Ellsworth's body lies a-mouldering in the grave
> As we go marching on.

And the Negro soldiers of the "First Arkansaw" used the same tune for their marching song:

> Oh, we're the bully soldiers of the First Arkansaw;
> We are fighting for de Union, we are fighting for de law.

The melody, with its stirring rhythms, represents the amalgam of Negro and white spirituals and Gospel tunes which has become our national music. Several of our former presidents hoped it would become our national anthem, and "The Battle Hymn of the Republic" did have this status unofficially, with a few of our other patriotic songs, until 1931, when Congress officially chose "The Star-Spangled Banner" for this honor.

# Battle Hymn of the Republic

Words: Julia Ward Howe
Music: William Steffe

lu - jah! Glo - ry! Glo - ry! Hal - le - lu - jah! His

truth is march - ing on._____ 2. I have on.

**2.**

I have seen Him in the watch-fires of a hundred circling camps;
They have builded Him an altar in the evening dews and damps;
I can read His righteous sentence by the dim and flaring lamps;
His day is marching on.

*Chorus*: Glory! Glory! etc.

**3.**

I have read a fiery gospel writ in burnish'd rows of steel;
"As ye deal with my contemners, so with you my grace shall deal;"
Let the Hero, born of woman, crush the serpent with his heel,
Since God is marching on.

*Chorus*: Glory! Glory! etc.

**4.**

He has sounded forth the trumpet that shall never call retreat;
He is sifting out the hearts of men before His judgment-seat;
Oh, be swift, my soul, to answer Him! be jubilant, my feet!
Our God is marching on.

*Chorus*: Glory! Glory! etc.

**5.**

In the beauty of the lilies Christ was born across the sea,
With a glory in His bosom that transfigures you and me:
As He died to make men holy, let us die to make men free,
While God is marching on.

*Chorus*: Glory! Glory! etc.

# John Brown's Body

John Brown was a "fanatical abolitionist." He planned to fortify himself in the southern mountains and fight against slavery with the aid of runaway Negroes. The attack he led on the government arsenal at Harper's Ferry, which was within the boundaries of West Virginia, was to get arms. Many of his fellow patriots were killed. John Brown was severely wounded and captured. He was tried, convicted of treason and hanged on December 2, 1859. In a note to his children he stated that he was as contented "to die for God's eternal truth on the scaffold as in any other way."

Although the abolitionist forces considered his actions as an attack on orderly government, his courage became legend. This tune has been called the "Marseillaise of Emancipation." (Same tune as "The Battle Hymn of the Republic")

**1.**
John Brown's body lies a-mouldering
    in the grave (repeat three times)
His soul is marching on.

*Chorus:*
    Glory, glory, hallelujah
    (repeat three times)
    His soul is marching on.

**2.**
The stars of heaven are looking kindly
    down (repeat three times)
On the grave of old John Brown.

*Chorus:* Glory, glory, etc.

**3.**
He's gone to be a soldier in the army of
    the Lord (repeat three times)
His soul is marching on.

*Chorus:* Glory, glory, etc.

**4.**
John Brown's knapsack is strapped upon
    his back (repeat three times)
His soul is marching on.

*Chorus:* Glory, glory, etc.

**5.**
His pet lambs will meet him on the
    way (repeat three times)
And they'll go marching on.

*Chorus:* Glory, glory, etc.

# Dixie's Land

Words and Music: ·
Dan Decatur Emmett

For their national rallying song the Southern people turned to the composition of a Northern composer, created numerous verses for it, made it the most parodied song of the war, and gave it a degree of immortality. The song is "Dixie," composed by Dan Decatur Emmett, and published in 1859. *

"Dixie" was written as a closing number for Bryant's Minstrels who were then performing in Mechanics Hall, New York. Carlo Patti, conductor of the orchestra at the Varieties Theatre in New Orleans introduced it to the South by using it in a march and drill routine by forty female Zouaves, and overnight it became the rage of the town. It was played in 1861 at the inauguration of Jefferson Davis as President of the Confederate States.

1. I wish I was in de land ob cot - ton, Old times dar am not for-got-ten look a - way, Look a - way! Look a - way! Dix - ie Land. In Dix - ie Land whar I was born in, Ear - ly on one

*Harwell, R.B., *Confederate Music*

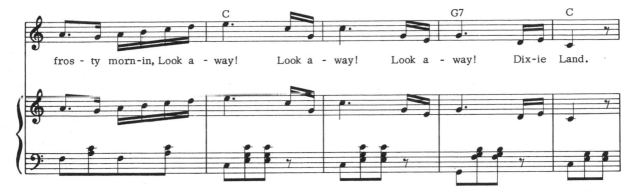

fros - ty morn-in, Look a - way! Look a - way! Look a - way! Dix-ie Land.

*Chorus*

Den I wish I was in Dix - ie, Hoo - ray! Hoo - ray! In____

Dix - ie Land, I'll took my stand, To lib an die in Dix - ie, A -

way, A - way, A - way down south in Dix - ie, A - way, A -

way, A - way down south in Dix - ie. 2. Old____ Dix - ie.

**2.**

Old Missus marry "Will-de-weaber,"
William was a gay deceaber;
    Look away! etc.
But when he put his arm around 'er
He smiled as fierce as a forty pounder.
    Look away! etc.

*Chorus*: Den I wish, etc.

**3.**

His face was sharp as a butcher's cleaber,
But dat did not seem to greab 'er;
    Look away! etc.
Old Missus acted de foolish part,
And died for a man dat broke her heart.
    Look away! etc.

*Chorus*: Den I wish, etc.

**4.**

Now here's a health to the next old Missus,
An all de gals dat want to kiss us;
    Look away! etc.
But if you want to drive 'way sorrow,
Come and hear dis song to-morrow,
    Look away! etc.

*Chorus*: Den I wish, etc.

**5.**

Dar's buck-wheat cakes an Ingen' batter,
Makes you fat or a little fatter;
    Look away! etc.
Den hoe it down and scratch your grabble.
To Dixie's land I'm bound to trabble,
    Look away! etc.

*Chorus*: Den I wish, etc.

# Everybody's Dixie
## (Selected Verses and Parodies)

This Southern version was written by General Albert Pike of Arkansas. He was Indian Commissioner to the Confederate Government and, curiously, a native of Vermont.

### 1.

Southrons, hear your country call you!
Up! lest worse than death befall you!
    To arms! to arms! to arms! in Dixie!
Lo! the beacon fire's lighted!
Let our hearts be now united!
    To arms! to arms! to arms! in Dixie!

*Chorus:*
    Advance the flag of Dixie!
      Hurrah! Hurrah!
    For Dixie's land we'll take our stand
      To live or die for Dixie!
      To arms! To arms!
    And conquer peace for Dixie!

### 2.

How the South's great heart rejoices
At your cannons' ringing voices!
    To arms! to arms! to arms! in Dixie!
For faith betrayed and pledges broken,
Wrongs inflicted, insults spoken.
    To arms! to arms! to arms! in Dixie!

*Chorus:* Advance the flag, etc.

### 3.

If the loved ones weep in sadness,
Victory shall bring them gladness;
    To arms! to arms! to arms! in Dixie!
Exultant pride soon banish sorrow;
Smiles chase tears away to-morrow.
    To arms! to arms! to arms! in Dixie!

*Chorus:* Advance the flag, etc.

And the Wolverines from Michigan showed their concern for the Stars and Stripes:

    Away down South where grows the cotton
    Seventy six seems quite forgotten
      Far away, far away, far away, Dixie land.
    And men with rebel shout and thunder
    Tear our good old flag asunder
      Far away, far away, far away, Dixie land.

"The Bucket-eers," members of Ward's legion in Texas, came up with this:

One night when we were getting dry,
A little old whiskey was the cry;
    Away, away, away, down South in Texas.
The boys hit up they had a plan,
To rob the commissary man,
    Away, away, away, down South in Texas.

*Chorus:*
O, when we get the whiskey, away, away,
We'll drink old rum, and think we're home
Away down South in Texas.
    Away, away, away, down South in Texas.
    Away, away, away, down South in Texas.

A soldier on the "mud march" after the battle of Fredericksburg sang:

    I wish I was in St. Law County
    Two years up and I had my bounty
    Away, look away, away, away. *

Perhaps "the hightoned gentlemen" enjoyed this quip:

    The ladies! Bless the darling creatures!
    Quite distort their pretty features,
      For the war, for the war, for the war, in Dixie.
    And say, I know you've seen it done sir,
    "They'll have an officer or none sir,"
      For the war, for the war, for the war, in Dixie.

*Wiley, B.I., *The Life of Billy Yank*, p. 162
Bobbs Merrill Co.

# The Flag of Columbia

Words and Music:
Harrison Millard

The favorite symbol for rallying allegiance on both sides of the struggle was the Stars and Stripes. Many songs appeared glorifying its virtues and the ideas it represented. Harrison Millard also composed "The Flag of the Free."

1. O, Land of Col - um - bia how glo - rious the sight, When __ mil - lions of free-men rise up in their might, To bat - tle for Un - ion and Lib - er - ty's cause And __ aid in de - fend - ing thy time hon - or'd laws: "The Un - ion it

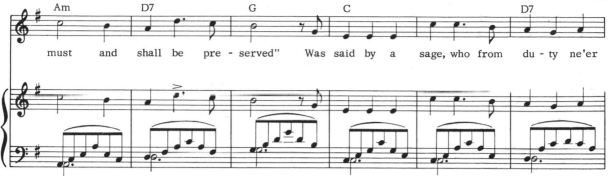

must and shall be pre-served" Was said by a sage, who from du-ty ne'er

swerved; So we say, let trai-tors de-cide what they__ will, The flag of Col-

um-bia shall float o'er us still, Shall__ float o'er us still, shall__ float o'er us

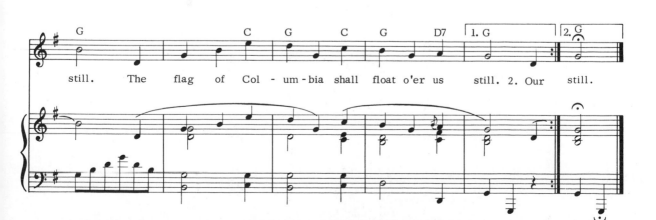

still. The flag of Col-um-bia shall float o'er us still. 2. Our still.

2.

Our watchword in battle, whenever we fight
Is "Freedom and Union" and "God speed the right;"
Each day brings us wisdom and strength to withstand
The whole world together, if foe to our land:
"United we stand, divided we fall"
Was said by a patriot well known to us all;
So we say, etc.

3.

The monarchs of Europe may well stand aghast,
And own that the day of their tyranny's past;
Oppression shall vanish and peoples be freed
They call on us now in the hour of their need:
"The Union of States th' enforcement of laws"
Will prove to the world that Heaven blesses our cause,
And we say, etc.

REPLACING THE FLAG ON SUMTER.

# The Bonnie Blue Flag

Words: Harry Macarthy
Music: "The Irish Jaunting Car"

Excluding "Dixie," the most popular song in the South and with the Confederate army was "The Bonnie Blue Flag." It was first presented by Marion Macarthy, sister of the author and "Arkansas comedian," at the Varieties Theatre in New Orleans for one of Harry's "Personation Acts." Troops en route to Virginia sang it at the New Orleans Academy of Music in September, 1861. The flag was displayed at the Mississippi Convention of January 9, 1861 which passed the act of secession, and the delegates chanted the new air. The words tell the story of secession and reveal the "temperament of the states at war" and invite other states to join in. The tune is an old Hibernian melody.

Brander Matthews tells us when General Butler was in command of New Orleans, he "made it very profitable by fining every man, woman or child who sang, whistled or played it on any instrument $25.00, besides arresting the publisher, destroying the sheet music and fining him $500."*

rah    for    the    Bon - nie Blue Flag,    that    bears    a    Sin - gle    Star!_____

**Chorus**

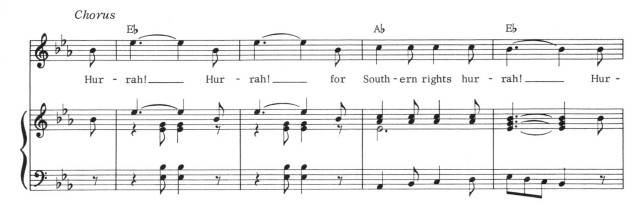

Hur - rah!_____    Hur - rah!_____    for    South - ern rights hur - rah!_____    Hur -

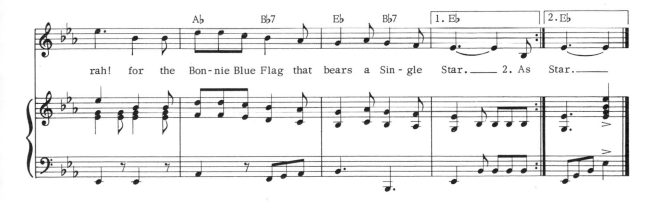

rah!    for    the    Bon - nie Blue Flag    that    bears    a    Sin - gle    Star.____ 2. As    Star._____

**2.**

As long as the Union was faithful to her trust,
Like friends and brethren kind were we, and just;
But now, when Northern treachery attempts our rights to mar,
We hoist on high the Bonnie Blue Flag that bears a single star.

*Chorus*: Hurrah, hurrah, etc.

**3.**

First gallant South Carolina nobly made the stand,
Then came Alabama and took her by the hand;
Next, quickly, Mississippi, Georgia, and Florida,
All raised on high the Bonnie Blue Flag that bears a single star.

*Chorus*: Hurrah, hurrah, etc.

**4.**

Ye men of valor gather round the banner of the right,
Texas and fair Louisiana join us in the fight;
With Davis, our loved President, and Stephens, statemen rare
We'll rally round the Bonnie Blue Flag that bears the single star.

*Chorus*: Hurrah, hurrah, etc.

**5.**

And here's to brave Virginia, the Old Dominion State,
With the young Confederacy at length has linked her faith;
Impelled by her example, now other States prepare
To hoist on high the Bonnie Blue Flag that bears a single star.

*Chorus*: Hurrah, hurrah, etc.

**6.**

Then cheer, boys, cheer, raise a joyous shout
For Arkansas and North Carolina now have both gone out,
And let another rousing cheer for Tennessee be given,
The single star of the Bonnie Blue Flag has grown to be eleven.

*Chorus*: Hurrah, hurrah, etc.

**7.**

Then here's to our Confederacy, strong we are and brave,
Like patriots of old we'll fight, our heritage to save;
And rather than submit to shame, to die we would prefer,
So cheer for the Bonnie Blue Flag that bears a single star.

*Chorus*: Hurrah, hurrah, etc.

# The Bonnie Blue Flag with the Stripes and Stars

Words: Col. J. L. Geddes
Music: "The Irish Jaunting Car"

The success of the song in the South soon invited parody from the North who came forth with a ready answer:

> Hurrah! hurrah! for equal rights hurrah!
> Hurrah! for the brave old flag that bears the Stripes and Stars.

While a prisoner of war in Selma, Alabama, Col. J. L. Geddes of the Eighth Iowa Infantry wrote "The Bonnie Blue Flag with the Stripes and Stars," and it was sung by members of his regiment in answer to the Southern song.

1.

We're fighting for our Union, we're fighting for our trust,
We're fighting for that happy land where sleeps our Father's dust.
It cannot be dissever'd, tho' it cost us bloody wars.
We never can give up the land where float the Stripes and Stars.

*Chorus:*
Hurrah! hurrah! for equal rights hurrah!
Hurrah! for the brave old flag that bears the Stripes and Stars.

2.

We treated you as brothers until you drew the sword,
With impious hands at Sumter you cut the silver cord,
So now you hear our bugles; we come the sons of Mars,
We rally round that brave old flag which bears the Stripes and Stars.

*Chorus:* Hurrah! hurrah! etc.

3.

We do not want your cotton, we care not for your slaves,
But rather than divide this land, we'll fill your southern graves.
With Lincoln for our Chieftain, we'll wear our country's scars.
We rally round that brave old flag that bears the Stripes and Stars!

*Chorus:* Hurrah! Hurrah! etc.

4.

We deem our cause most holy, we know we're in the right,
And twenty millions of freemen stand ready for the fight.
Our bride is fair Columbia, no stain her beauty mars.
O'er her we'll raise that brave old flag which bears the Stripes and Stars

*Chorus:* Hurrah! hurrah! etc.

5.

And when this war is over, we'll each resume our home
And treat you still as brothers where ever you may roam.
We'll pledge the hand of friendship, and think no more of wars,
But dwell in peace beneath the flag that bears the Stripes and Stars!

*Chorus:* Hurrah! hurrah! etc.

# Dixie, The Land of King Cotton

Words: Capt. Hughes
Music: John Hill Hewitt

This song is from Hewitt's military operetta, "The Vivandiere," which contains many military and spirited patriotic songs. The operetta also describes camp scenes and the bustle of war. Hewitt's songs and stage works were very popular at the time. A native of New York, at the time of the war he was training troops in Virginia.

1. Oh,— Dix - ie the land of King Cot-ton, The— home of the brave and the

free; A— na - tion by Free-dom be - got-ten, The ter - ror of des - pots to

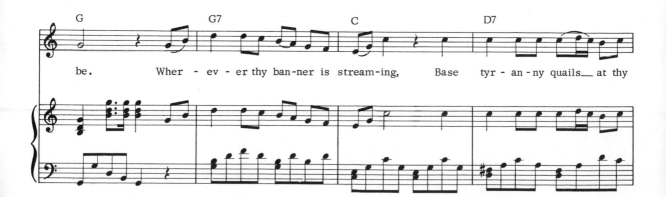

be. Wher - ev - er thy ban-ner is stream-ing, Base tyr - an - ny quails— at thy

feet;  And Lib-er-ty's sun-light is beam-ing  In splen-dor of ma - jes-ty sweet.

*Chorus*

Then three cheers for our ar - my so true, Three cheers for our pres-i-dent— too; May our

ban-ner tri-um-phant-ly wave—  O-ver Dix-ie, the land— of the brave!  brave!

**2.**

When Liberty sounds her war rattle,
Demanding her right and her due;
The first land that rallies to battle
Is Dixie, the home of the true.
Thick as leaves of the forest in summer,
Her brave sons will rise on each plain;
And then strike till each Vandal comer
Lies dead on the soil he would stain.

*Chorus*: Then three cheers, etc.

**3.**

May the names of the dead that we cherish,
Fill memory's cup to the brim;
May the laurels we've won never perish,
Nor our stars of their glory grow dim.
May the States of the South never sever,
But companions of Freedom e'er be;
May they flourish Confed'rate forever,
The boast of the brave and the free.

*Chorus*: Then three cheers, etc.

# Maryland, My Maryland

Words: James Ryder Randall
Music: "Tannenbaum, O Tannenbaum"

The poem was written by James Ryder Randall, a native of Baltimore. It was on April 23, 1861, when the poet was only twenty-two years old and a professor of English literature at Poydras College at Point Coupée, Louisiana, that he read in the New Orleans Delta the news of the attack of troops of the Sixth Massachusetts Regiment as they passed through his native city. "The account excited me greatly," Randall wrote to Brander Matthews. "That night I could not sleep. About midnight I arose, lit a candle, and went to my desk. Some powerful spirit appeared to possess me, and almost involuntarily I proceeded to write the song of 'My Maryland'."*

The poem received its musical wings through the ingenuity of Miss Hetty Cary and her musically talented sister, Jenny. They discovered that the tune "Lauriger Horatius," long a favorite college song, fitted the new lyric perfectly. The union of tune and poem sparked the camp fires of the Southern armies. According to Harwell, this song was "only a little less popular than Dixie."** The tune stems from an old German air, "Tannenbaum, O Tannenbaum," which Longfellow translated as "My Hemlock Tree."

1. The des-pot's heel is on thy shore, Ma-ry-land, my Ma-ry-land! His torch is at thy tem-ple door, Ma-ry-land, my Ma-ry-land! A- venge the pa - tri - ot - ic gore That flecked the streets of Bal - ti-more, And

*Matthews, B., *Pen and Ink*
**Harwell, R.B., *Confederate Music*

be the bat - tle queen of yore, Ma - ry-land, my Ma - ry-land! 2. Hark Ma - ry-land!

**2.**
Hark to an exiled son's appeal,
    Maryland, my Maryland!
My mother State, to thee I kneel,
    Maryland, my Maryland!
For life or death, for woe or weal,
Thy peerless chivalry reveal,
And gird they beauteous limbs with steel,
    Maryland, my Maryland!

**3.**
Thou wilt not cower in the dust,
    Maryland, my Maryland!
Thy beaming sword shall never rust,
    Maryland, my Maryland!
Remember Carroll's sacred trust.
Remember Howard's warlike thrust,
And all thy slumberers with the just,
    Maryland, my Maryland!

**4.**
Come! 'tis the red dawn of the day,
    Maryland, my Maryland!
Come with thy panoplied array,
    Maryland, my Maryland!
With Ringgold's spirit for the fray,
With Watson's blood at Monterey,
With fearless Lowe and dashing May,
    Maryland, my Maryland!

**5.**
Dear mother, burst the tyrant's chain,
    Maryland, my Maryland!
Virginia should not call in vain,
    Maryland, my Maryland!
She meets her sisters on the plain,
"Sic semper!" 'tis the proud refrain
That baffles minions back amain,
    Maryland, my Maryland!
Arise in majesty again,
    Maryland, my Maryland!

**6.**
Come! for thy shield is brighter and strong,
    Maryland, my Maryland!
Come! for thy dalliance does thee wrong,
    Maryland, my Maryland!
Come to thine own heroic throng,
Stalking with liberty along,
And chant thy dauntless slogan-song,
    Maryland, my Maryland!

**7.**
I see the blush upon thy cheek,
    Maryland, my Maryland!
But thou wast ever bravely meek,
    Maryland, my Maryland!
But lo! there surges forth a shriek,
From hill to hill, from creek to creek,
Potomac calls to Chesapeake,
    Maryland, my Maryland!

**8.**
Thou wilt not yield the vandal toll,
    Maryland, my Maryland!
Thou wilt not crook to his control,
    Maryland, my Maryland!
Better the fire upon the roll,
Better the shot, the blade, the bowl,
Than crucifixion of the soul,
    Maryland, my Maryland!

**9.**
I hear the distant thunder-bum,
    Maryland, my Maryland!
The "Old Line's" bugle, fife, and drum,
    Maryland, my Maryland!
She is not dead, nor deaf, nor dumb;
Huzza! she spurns the Northern scum —
She breathes! She burns! She'll come! She'll come!
    Maryland, my Maryland

# Maryland, My Maryland
## (A Northern Reply)

The rousing spirit of the song invited answers from the North. Sep Winner, a very successful song writer of Civil War songs composed this fervent reply.

### 1.

The Rebel horde is on thy shore,
    Maryland! My Maryland!
Arise and drive him from thy door,
    Maryland! My Maryland!
Avenge the foe thou must abhor
Who seeks thy fall, Oh Baltimore,
Drive back the tyrant, peace restore,
    Maryland, My Maryland!

### 2.

Hark to a nation's warm appeal,
Maryland! My Maryland!
And sister states that for thee feel,
    Maryland, My Maryland!
Gird now thy sons with arms of steel,
And heavy be the blows they deal,
For traitors shall thy vengeance feel,
    Maryland, My Maryland!

### 3.

Thou wilt not cower in the dust,
    Maryland! My Maryland!
Thy gleaming sword shall never rust,
    Maryland! My Maryland!
Thy sons shall battle with the just
And soon repel the traitor's thrust,
For in their strength our state shall trust,
    Maryland! My Maryland!

### 4.

Come! for thy men are bold and strong,
    Maryland! My Maryland!
Drive back the foe that would thee wrong,
    Maryland! My Maryland!
Come with thine own heroic throng,
And as thy army moves along,
Let Union be their constant song,
    Maryland! My Maryland!

### 5.

Virginia feels the tyrant's chain,
    Maryland! My Maryland!
Her children lie around her slain,
    Maryland! My Maryland!
Let Carolina call in vain,
Our rights we know and will maintain,
Our rise shall be her fall again,
    Maryland! My Maryland!

### 6.

I hear the distant battles hum,
    Maryland! My Maryland!
I hear the bugle, fife and drum,
    Maryland! My Maryland!
Thou art not deaf, thou art not dumb,
Thou wilt not falter nor succumb,
I hear thee cry we come, we come!
    Maryland! My Maryland!

### 7.

Ten hundred thousand, brave and free,
    Maryland! My Maryland!
Are ready now to strike with thee,
    Maryland! My Maryland!
A Million more still yet agree,
To help thee hold thy liberty,
For thou shalt ever ever be,
    Maryland! My Maryland!

# Emancipation

Words and Music:
Anonymous

Lincoln drafted the Emancipation Proclamation in July, 1862. After waiting for the propitious time, he released it to the nation on September 22, 1862 as a "necessary war measure" to become effective January 1, 1863. This song was published in 1864 and makes a fervent appeal for abolition and freedom. It warns that "Despots will feel that Republican steel is sharp in defence of the nation." The Thirteenth Amendment, constitutionally abolishing slavery, was ratified in 1865, and the conquered states accepted it after the war.

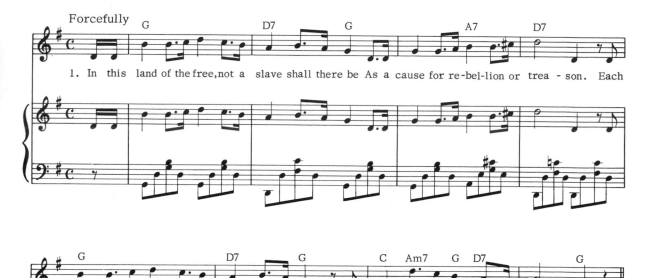

1. In this land of the free, not a slave shall there be As a cause for re-bel-lion or trea - son. Each

fet - ter and chain in the sod shall be lain, For this, if for no oth - er rea - son.

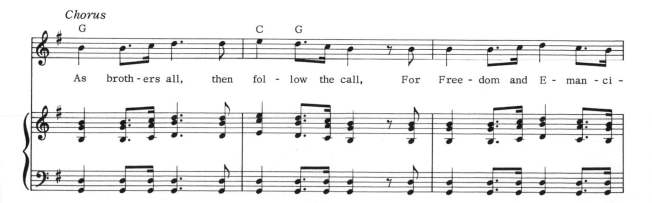

*Chorus*

As broth - ers all, then fol - low the call, For Free - dom and E - man - ci -

pa - tion, A man is a man, de - ny it who can, It shall

be so at least in this na - tion. na - tion.

### 2.
O, who is so vile as to linger and smile
When a man to the slave pen is driven,
And sold like a beast, his poor body at least,
Tho' his soul may be ransomed in Heaven.

*Chorus*: As brothers all, etc.

### 3.
With the blood of the slain, we will wipe out the stain
Which forced men to blush for this nation
That bartered and sold men and women for gold
Who oft were of kindred relation.

*Chorus*: As brothers all, etc.

### 4.
A white slave or black, is a man for all that,
Tho' the law may deny him his station,
The birth-right of all is to join in the call
For God and for Emancipation.

*Chorus*: As brothers all, etc.

### 5.
We offer the hand to all in this land
Who are fighting for our preservation,
Upholding just laws and Freedoms' great cause
And the Union of all this great nation.

*Chorus*: As brothers all, etc.

### 6.
The nation shall grow and to other lands show,
This Republic is firm in foundation,
And Despots shall feel that republican steel,
Is sharp in defence of this nation.

*Chorus*: As brothers all, etc.

### 7.
This land of the free still a refuge shall be
For all the oppress'd who are driven
To exile from home, to as many as come,
To each an asylum is given.

*Chorus*: As brothers all, etc.

### 8.
Then join in the cry till it reaches the sky,
And there is recorded forever,
There'll not be a slave, in this "home of the brave"
If there is, we his fetters will sever.

*Chorus*: As brothers all, etc.

# May God Save the Union

Words: Rev. G. Douglass Brewerton
Music: Carl Wolfsohn

The Union hymn combines patriotism with a stoic religious dignity. The lyrics sing and pray that the "stars of our flag will tell of a glorious past and bind us in Union for ever to last."

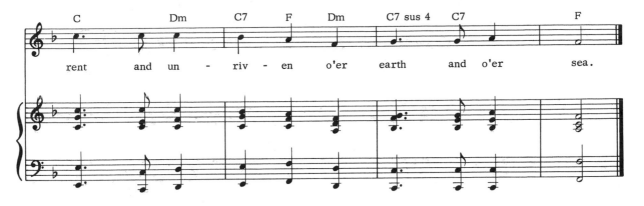

rent and un - riv - en o'er earth and o'er sea.

2.

May God save the Union! We trust in its might,
In time of the tempest, in fear and in flight,
We'll fail not, we'll faint not if still in the sky
We see all the stars in the azure field fly.

3.

May God save the Union! Still, still may it stand
Upheld by the strength of the patriot hand,
To cement it our fathers ensanguined the sod,
To keep it we kneel to a merciful God.

4.

May God save the Union! The Red, White and Blue,
Our States keep united the dreary day through,
Let the stars tell the tale of the glorious past
And bind us in Union forever to last.

# God Save the South

Words: Earnest Halphin
Music: Charles W. A. Ellerbrock

This hymn was very popular during Confederate times. The lyrics and music reveal the religious spirit of faith and devotion to the rightness of the struggle. It was one of the first songs to be published during the war.

God save the South, God save the South, Her al - tars and

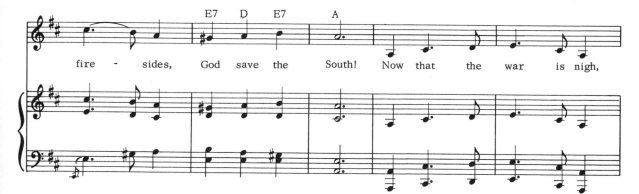

fire - sides, God save the South! Now that the war is nigh,

Now that we arm to die, Chant - ing our bat - tle cry, Free - dom or

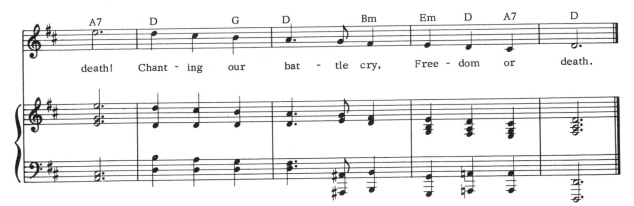

death! Chant - ing our bat - tle cry, Free - dom or death.

**2.**

God be our shield,
At home or afield,
Stretch thine arm over us,
Strengthen and save.
What tho' they're three to one,
Forward each sire and son,
Strike till the war is won,
Strike to the grave!

**3.**

God made the right,
Stronger than might,
Millions would trample us
Down in their pride.
Lay Thou their legions low,
Roll back the ruthless foe.
Let the proud spoiler know
God's on our side.

**4.**

Hark honor's call,
Summoning all,
Summoning all of us
Unto the strife.
Sons of the South awake!
Strike till the brand shall break,
Strike for dear Honor's sake.
Freedom and Life!

**5.**

Rebels before
Our fathers of yore,
Rebel's the righteous name
Washington bore.
Why, then, be ours the same.
The name that he snatch'd from shame,
Making it first in fame,
Foremost in war.

**6.**

War to the hilt,
Theirs be the guilt,
Who fetter the free man
To ransom the slave.
Up then, and undismay'd,
Sheathe not the battle blade
Till the last foe is laid
Low in the grave!

**7.**

God save the South
God save the South,
Dry the dim eyes that now
Follow our path.
Still let the light feet rove
Safe through the orange grove;
Still keep the land we love
Safe from Thy wrath.

**8.**

God save the South,
God save the South,
Her altars and firesides,
God save the South!
For the great war is nigh,
And we will win or die,
Chaunting our battle cry,
Freedom or death!

# Strike for the South

Words: Carrie Bell Sinclair
Music: James Pierpont

After the Confederate defeat at Gettysburg and with the Union pouring fresh manpower into the field, the South needed a new patriotic "shot in the arm." Miss Sinclair, an Augusta poetess, responded with this proud and stirring lyric. She contributed frequently to Confederate literary periodicals, notably "The Southern Field and Fireside."*

*Harwell, R. B., *Confederate Music*

wave. _____ Strike for the South! shall the he - roes who

fell, In graves all un - hon - or'd re - pose, _____ While the

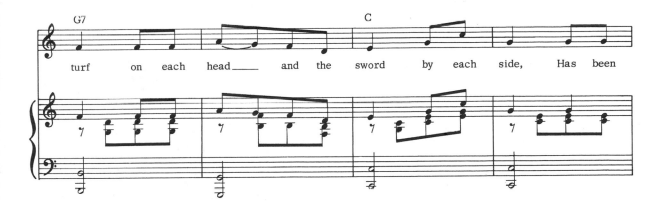

turf on each head \_\_\_\_ and the sword by each side, Has been

stain'd with the blood \_\_\_ of her foes. _____ show. _____

2.

Strike for the South! we will honor her name
For the glorious deeds she has done!
The laurel we'll twine 'round each patriot brow,
And shout when the battle is won.
Strike for the South! it must never be said
That her banner was furl'd to a foe;
Let those stars ever shine in bright glory above,
And the pathway to victory show.

3.

Strike for the South! for Liberty's sun
In darkness and gloom has not set;
Her bright beams still shine like a light from above,
And will lead thee to victory yet.
Strike for the South! for her weapons are bright,
And the heroes who wield them are strong;
Let her name brightly glow on the record of fame,
And hers be the proudest in song.

# Battle Cry of Freedom
## (Rallying Song)

Words and Music:
George F. Root

This was one of Root's best songs. It was the most effective rallying song of the North. Soldiers sang it in battle, in camps and on the long march. The naturalness and spontaneity in the melody and rhythm give it those national qualities of a patriotic song. Root composed two sets of verses, one a civilian "rallying" song, the second a battle song. The Confederates could not resist the flavor of this spirited tune. One of their prolific composers, H. L. Schreiner, adapted Root's tune for a patriotic song with words by W. H. Barnes.

1. Yes we'll ral - ly 'round the flag, boys, we'll ral - ly once a - gain,

Shout - ing the bat - tle cry of Free - dom, We will ral - ly from the hill - side, we'll

gath - er from the plain, Shout - ing the bat - tle cry of Free - dom.

**2.**
We are springing to the call
Of our brothers gone before,
   Shouting the battle cry of Freedom,
And we'll fill the vacant ranks
With a million Free men more,
   Shouting the battle cry of Freedom.

*Chorus*

**3.**
We will welcome to our numbers
The loyal, true and brave,
   Shouting the battle cry of Freedom,
And although he may be poor
He shall never be a slave,
   Shouting the battle cry of Freedom.

*Chorus*

**4.**
So we're springing to the call
From the East and from the West,
   Shouting the battle cry of Freedom,
And we'll hurl the rebel crew
From the land we love the best,
   Shouting the battle cry of Freedom.

*Chorus*

# Battle Cry of Freedom

## Southern Version

**1.**

Our flag is proudly floating
On the land and on the main,
    Shout, shout, the battle cry of Freedom;
Beneath it oft we've conquered
And will conquer oft again,
    Shout, shout, the battle cry of Freedom.

*Chorus:*

    Our Dixie forever, she's never at a loss
    Down with the eagle and up with the cross.
    We'll rally 'round the bonny flag, we'll rally once again.
    Shout, shout the battle cry of Freedom.

**2.**

Our gallant boys have marched
To the rolling of the drums,
    Shout, shout the battle cry of Freedom;
And the leaders in charge
Cry, "Come boys, come!"
    Shout, shout the battle cry of Freedom.

*Chorus:*   Our Dixie forever, etc.

**3.**

They have laid down their lives
On the bloody battle field,
    Shout, shout, the battle cry of Freedom;
Their motto is resistance —
"To tyrants we'll not yield!"
    Shout, shout the battle cry of Freedom.

*Chorus:* Our Dixie forever, etc.

**4,**

While our boys have responded
And to the field have gone,
    Shout, shout the battle cry of Freedom;
Our noble women also
Have aided them at home.
    Shout, shout the battle cry of Freedom.

*Chorus:* Our Dixie forever, etc.

# Virginia Marseillaise

Words: F. W. Rosier
Music: Rouget de L'isle

The French population in New Orleans inspired many patriotic songs. In his "Confederate Music," R. B. Harwell comments on a manuscript by John Hill Hewitt which reports that the enduring hymn was sung by the Louisiana Creoles in 1812 and later spread to the Confederate armies. It is also recorded that the song was so completely identified with the South that a foreign troupe who sang it in a New York theatre "were thrown into prison as suspected secessionists." The hymn was also published as "La Louisianaise" and "The Southern Marseillaise."

The Union could not resist the stirring strains and came out with the "Northmen's Marseillaise."

"Ye sons of Freedom, wake to glory!
Hark! hark! what thousands bid you rise!"*

*Harwell, R. B., *Confederate Music*, p. 62

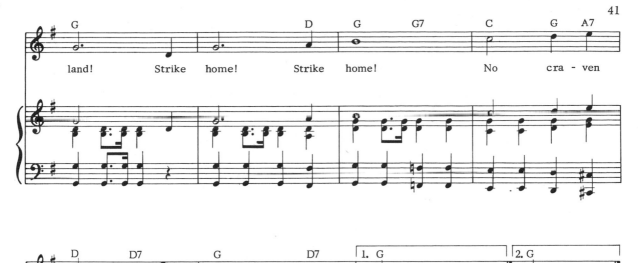

land! Strike home! Strike home! No cra-ven

fear! For home and na-tive land! 2. Shall the land!

**2.**

Shall the sons of Old Virginia
　　Prove unworthy of their sires?
No! they'll show the haughty foeman
　　That in fight, she "never tires,"
With fav'ring Heaven to befriend her.
　　To whom alone she bends the knee,
　　'Till every foot of soil is free,
She her sacred cause will ne'er surrender.
　　To arms! etc.

**3.**

A ray of never dying glory
　　Shall Virginia's brow o'erspread;
Men unborn shall tell the story,
　　How their fathers fought and bled,
While fairest hands their wounds were tending.
　　And brightest eyes the dear bewailed,
　　How not a noble bosom quailed,
E'en to die, their native land defending.
　　To arms! etc.

**4.**

O Liberty! can man resign thee,
　　Who has felt thy gen'rous flame?
Can dungeons, bolts and bars confine thee,
　　Or whips thy noble spirit tame?
Too long the world has wept, bewailing
　　The savage pow'r that conquerors wield,
　　But Freedom is our sword and shield,
And all their arts are unavailing.
　　To arms! etc.

**5.**

Long be it thus, may we forever
　　For Freedom brave the battle storm;
Rise in her might, and rising, sever
　　The bonds that tyrant bands would form.
Then plume and steel in sunbeams glancing,
　　Shall show where Freedom's banners float,
　　And thrilling to the trumpet's note,
We'll see her warrior sons advancing.
　　To arms! etc.

# Melt the Bells

Words: J. V. Rockett
Music: Mrs. Dr. Byrne

This song was published for the benefit of the Southern Relief Association by Balmer & Weber of St. Louis, Missouri. In the 1866 edition the following entry appeared:

> "In the first year of the Southern war, an order was issued by General Beauregard, to have the bells in the State of Louisiana melted into cannon. Many of the church bells and hundreds of plantation bells were sent to New Orleans for that purpose but unfortunately they were seized by General Butler and sent to Boston, where they still remain."

Although the South responded generously, it is still a matter of conjecture as to whether the cannons used in the Southland were made from the bells.

1. Melt the bells! Melt the bells! Still the tink - ling___ on the plain;

Melt the bells! Melt the bells! And trans - mute the eve - ning chimes In - to

war's re - sound - ing rhymes, That th'in - vad - er may be slain By the bells!

By the bells! That th'in - vad - er may be slain, By the bells! time 'Neath the bells.

**2.**
Melt the bells! melt the bells!
Though it cause a tear to part,
Melt the bells! melt the bells!
With the music they have made,
Where the ones we loved are laid
With pale cheek and silent heart,
'Neath the bells! 'neath the bells!
With pale cheek and silent heart
'Neath the bells.

**3.**
Melt the bells! melt the bells!
That for years have called for prayer
Melt the bells! melt the bells!
And instead the cannon's roar
Shall resound the valleys o'er
That the foe may catch despair
From the bells! from the bells!
That the foe may catch despair
From the bells.

**4.**
Melt the bells! melt the bells!
Into cannon rash and grim,
Melt the bells! melt the bells!
That the foe may feel the ire
From their heaving lungs of fire;
And we'll put our trust in Him
And the bells! and the bells!
And we'll put our trust in Him
And the bells.

**5.**
Melt the bells! melt the bells!
And when the foe are driven back,
Melt the bells! melt the bells!
And the lightning cloud of war
Shall roll thunderless afar
We will melt the cannon back,
Into bells! Into bells!
We will melt the cannon back
Into bells.

**6.**
Melt the bells! melt the bells!
And they'll peel a sweeter chime,
Melt the bells! melt the bells!
And remind us of the brave
Who have sunk to glory's grave
And who sleep for coming time
'Neath the bells! 'neath the bells!
And who sleep for coming time
'Neath the bells.

# Wait for the Wagon

Words and Music:
R. P. Buckley

The composer was a member of the Buckley Serenaders, a very popular Minstrel Troupe. This catchy tune was composed during the 1850's, and at the time of the war both sides realized it had excellent possibilities for parodies and lampoons. Many thousands rode the "wagon", and as they rolled along they chanted and made up rhymes for the cause as each side saw it at the time. Here are the original lyrics and some selected parodies.

1. Will you come with me, my Phyl - is dear, to yon Blue Moun - tain

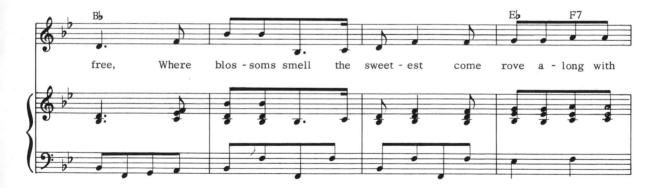

free, Where blos - soms smell the sweet - est come rove a - long with

me; It's ev - ry Sun day morn ing, when I am by your

side, We'll jump in - to the wag - on and all take a ride.

*Chorus*

Wait for the wag - on, wait for the wag - on,

Wait for the wag - on and we'll all take a ride. ride.

2.

Where the river runs like silver
And the birds they sing so sweet,
I have a cabin, Phyllis,
And something good to eat;
Come listen to my story,
It will relieve my heart;
So jump into the wagon,
And off we will start.
*Chorus*. Wait for the wagon, etc.

3.

Do you believe, my Phyllis, dear,
Old Mike, with all his wealth,
Can make you half so happy
As I, with youth and health?
We'll have a little farm,
A horse, a pig and cow;
And you will mind the dairy,
While I do guide the plough.
*Chorus*: Wait for the wagon, etc.

4.

Your lips are red as poppies,
Your hair so slick and neat,
All braided up with dahlias,
And hollyhocks so sweet.
It's ev'ry Sunday morning,
When I am by your side,
We'll jump into the wagon,
And all take a ride.
*Chorus*: Wait for the wagon, etc.

5.

Together, on life's journey,
We'll travel till we stop,
And if we have no trouble,
We'll reach the happy top;
Then come with me, sweet Phyllis,
My dear, my lovely bride,
We'll jump into the wagon,
And all take a ride.
*Chorus*: Wait for the wagon, etc.

# Wait for the Wagon
## A Northern Parody
The Union Wagon Couldn't Be Split

There's none can smash the wagon,
    'tis patented and strong,
And built of pure devotion,
    by those who hate the wrong;
Its wheels are made of freedom,
    which patriots adore,
The spokes when rightly counted,
    just number forty-four.

*Chorus:*
Keep in the wagon
The Old Union Wagon
The oft tested wagon
While millions take a ride.

## A Southern Parody

The Southern Wagon was "Respectfully dedicated and hitched up for the President, officers and men of the Confederate Army," and was written when only seven states were "on the wagon."

### 1.
Secession is our watchword,
    Our rights we will demand;
To defend our homes and firesides,
    We pledge our hearts and hand.
Jeff Davis is our President,
    With Stephen by our side;
Brave Beauregard, our General,
    Will join in our ride.

*Chorus:*
    Oh, wait for the wagon
    The Dissolution wagon;
    The South is our wagon
    And we'll all take a ride.

### 2.
Our wagon is the very best,
    The running gear is good;
Stuffed 'round the sides with cotton,
    And made of Southern wood.
Carolina is the driver,
    With Georgia by her side,
Virginia holds the flag up,
    While we all take a ride.

*Chorus:* Oh, wait, etc.

# A Southern Parody - continued

### 3.

There was Tennessee and Texas,
    Also in the ring;
They wouldn't have a government,
    Where cotton wasn't king.
Alabama and Florida
    Have long ago replied;
Mississippi and Louisiana
    Are anxious for the ride.

*Chorus:* Oh, wait, etc.

# A Northern Parody

The North sallied that the "Union Wagon" was built of sturdier stuff.

The makers of our wagon
    Were men of solid wit,
They made it out of Charter Oak
    Which would not be split;
Its wheels are of material,
    The strongest and the best.
And two are named the North and South,
    And two the East and West.

*Chorus:*

Hurrah for the wagon
The Old Union Wagon
We'll stick to our wagon
And all take a ride.

# A Southern Parody

Will Shakespeare Hays itemized the progress of secession:

### 1.
Jeff Davis built a wagon,
    And on it put his name,
And Beauregard was driver
    Of secession's ugly frame.
The horse he would get hungry,
    As most horses do,
They had to keep the collar tight
    To keep from pulling through.


*Chorus:*
    Bully, for the wagon,
    The new secession wagon;
    Oh, Beaury hold the nag in,
    While you all take a ride.

### 2.
The axles wanted greasing;
    The body wasn't wide.
North Carolina jumped into it,
    Mississippi by her side;
Virginia took a cushioned seat,
    And Louisiana next,
South Carolina got to scrounging
    And Florida got vexed.

*Chorus:* Bully, for the wagon, etc.

### 3.
They asked Kentucky to take a ride,
    She said the horse was blind;
She shook her head at seeing
    Tennessee jump on behind.
But Jeff assured her all was right,
    The wagon it was new,
Missouri winked at Beauregard;
    And said "it would not do."

*Chorus:* Bully, for the wagon, etc.

# Politics

# The Abe - iad

Words: J. P. McRebel
Music: F. Bartenstein

Political lampooning was an active practice with both sides. Lincoln and Davis received a good share of ribbing and castigation in song. At times the rhymes got pretty rough. The pen name of McRebel reveals the spirit of those politicians who were opposed to the cause of abolition.

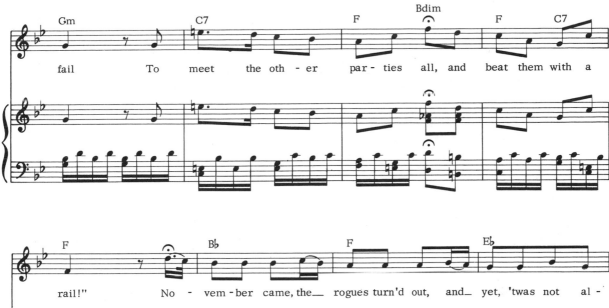

fail   To   meet   the   oth - er   par - ties   all,   and   beat   them   with   a

rail!"   No - vem - ber   came, the__ rogues turn'd out,   and__ yet, 'twas   not   al -

low'd,   That   Abe should come, lest   Ab- ram's   face, should fright a - way   the   crowd!   The

crowd,   the   crowd,   should   fright   a - way   the   crowd.   see.

### 2.

So Abram, at his Springfield home,
    Staid waiting for the news,
The while, his party lick'd their chops
    At smell of public stews;
Seen  hordes of ev'ry grade and shape,
    High, low, and ragged  feller
Came for each place, from Chair of State,
    To toting Abe's "Umbreller!"
So Abram, left, and foolish speech,
    And maudlin kiss and shout
Of flatt'ring rabble, well compos'd
    The triumph of his route!
His route, his route,
    The triumph of his route!

### 3.

At length, a man full hard he ran, -
    "A plot, a plot!" did yell,
Then quick beneath each seat they sought
    Infernal bursting shell;
The man, they tried (and faith he lied!)
    "The special train" he said
"Will be upset, and if Abe 'scapes,
    Arm'd men will shoot him dead!"
Abe's friends a counterplot did hatch,
    'Twas: "Run, Abe Lincoln, straight -
For running was a stratagem,
    Of Bonaparte, the Great!
The great, the great,
    Of Bonaparte, the Great!

### 4.

Away went Abram, meek or naught,
    All in the midnight dark!
Away went Abram, fast he flew!
    No Judge that time could mark!
And, dreading still, Grimalkin's corpse,
    Or brickbat's envious blow,
At dead of night, he slyly pass'd
    Thro' dreadful Baltimo'!
So Abe stole into Washington,
    (Alas! the woeful day,)
And fondly thought, poor foolish Abe!
    "Well, four years here I'll stay!
I'll stay, I'll stay,
    Well, four years here I'll stay!"

### 5.

Abe, human hopes are sandy ropes,
    To my advice give heed!
And dearly prize those lengthy limbs,
    Which give you wondrous speed!
Repent and change! or as you came,
    Soon darkly back you'll run;
Aye! day and night, with all your might,
    You'll run from sun to sun!
So let us say, make haste the day!
    And Abram, make haste he!
And when old Abe  shall run that race,
    May I be there to see!
To see, to see,
    May I be there to see!

# Call 'em Names, Jeff

Words: R. Tompkins
Music: Wurzel (George F. Root)

After the battles of the Wilderness, Spotsylvania and Cold Harbor, the Confederate forces began to dwindle. In order to discredit Lincoln, the Southerners encouraged the abolitionist label, and the North sallied with a tease: "If you can't beat 'em in battle, call 'em names."

1. Said Beau - re - gard, to Lee, and Jeff, "These Yan - kee sons of thun - der Will

scat - ter us from right to left, Or cause us to knock un - der, Un -

less we find some oth - er way Of meet - ing their ad - van - ces; we've

made up fa - ces now so long, They do not mind our glan - ces."

*Chorus*

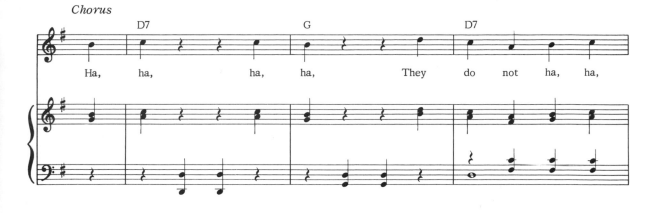

Ha, ha, ha, ha, They do not ha, ha,

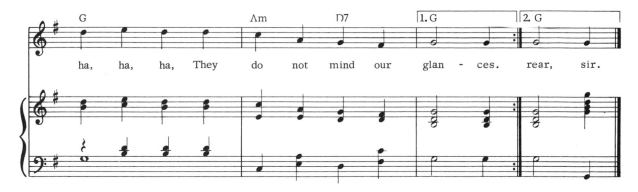

ha, ha, ha, They do not mind our glan - ces. rear, sir.

2.

"O true," said Jeff, "I know it well,
  How shall we change our game, sir,"
"O dear," said Lee, "I cannot tell,"
  Quoth Beau, "We'll call 'em names, sir."
"That's good," said Jeff. "You've hit it Beau."
  Cried Lee, "That's what's the matter;"
"We'll call them 'Abolitionists,'
  And then you'll see them scatter."

*Chorus*: Ha, ha, ha, ha, And then you'll —
      ha, ha, ha, ha, ha,
      And then you'll see them scatter.

3.

They really thought that calling names
    Had strengthen'd their position,
When all their sneaking curs up North
    Ran yelping Abolition;
But soon we made the traitors know
    'Twas something else the matter,
The more they 'Abolition' howl'd
    The more we did not scatter.

*Chorus*:  Ha, ha, ha, ha, The more we —
        ha, ha, ha, ha, ha,
        The more we did not scatter.

4.

We take the name you give us, Beau,
    We're forced to make it true, sir.
We'll first abolish Slavery's power,
    And then abolish you, sir.
When that is done, we'll home return,
    The home to us so dear, sir,
And soundly kick and cuff the curs,
    Now barking in our rear, sir.

*Chorus*:  Ha, ha, ha, ha, Now barking —
        ha, ha, ha, ha, ha,
        Now barking in our rear, sir.

# What's the Matter?

Words and Music:
Charles Boynton

While the troops fought it out on the battle field, Lincoln had to contend with opposing factions behind the lines. This song tells about the trouble caused by one of these disloyal groups, the Copperheads, who opposed the cause of the Union and fought Republican rule.

1. See the peo - ple turn - ing out, What, what's the mat - ter?

What is all this noise a - bout, What, what's the mat - ter?

Gath - er'd in from far and near, Ev - 'ry loy - al man is here,

What is it the peo - ple fear? What, What's the mat - ter?

*Chorus*

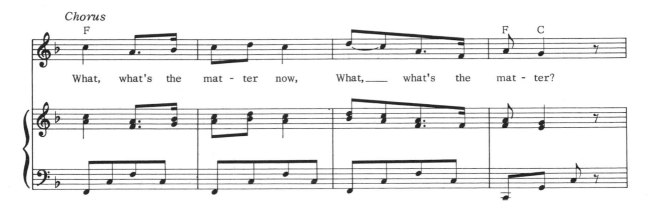

What, what's the mat - ter now, What,___ what's the mat - ter?

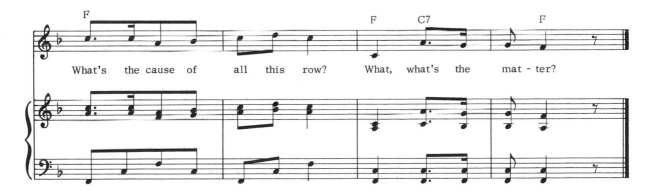

What's the cause of all this row? What, what's the mat - ter?

### 2.

Traitors in our midst we've found,
 That's what's the matter,
Peddling here their treason round,
 That's what's the matter,
Men that to our foes have cried,
 "You can count us on your side,
We will let the Union slide,"
 That's what's the matter.

*Chorus*:

 That's what's the matter now,
 That's what's the matter;
 Treason here we won't allow,
 That's what's the matter!

### 3.

Firing on our armies' rear —
  Trying to scatter
Disaffection far and near;
  That's what's the matter,
"Take your proclamation back;
  Take your armies off the track,"
Cry aloud this tory pack;
  That's what's the matter!

*Chorus*:

  That's what's the matter now,
  That's what's the matter;
  Treason here we won't allow,
  That's what's the matter.

### 4.

Hear ye what the people say,
  "Stop now your clatter;
Uncle Sam shall win the day;
  That's what's the matter
If he wants a million men
  Let him tell us where, and when,
They'll be ready there, and then;"
  That's what's the matter.

*Chorus*:

  That's what's the matter, ho!
  That's what's the matter -
  Every drafted man shall go,
  That's what's the matter.

A FAMILY QUARREL.

# Sister Carrie
## or
## The Compromise Song

Words and Music:
A. P. Peck

Neither the compromise of 1850 nor the Crittenden Proposal of 1860 could halt the tide of secession and war. This song is a "kiss and make up" lyric. Here is a plea to South Carolina to stick with the Union.

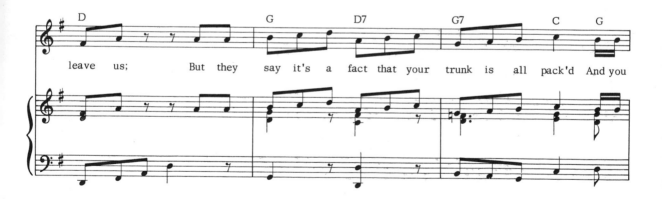

grieve us, dear Car - rie, You hope by such con - duct to grieve us.

**2.**
You have always been naughty,
And wilful and haughty;
Like a spoiled little minx as you are,
So vain of your beauty,
Forgetful of duty,
You owe to indulgent papa.

*Chorus*:
   You owe to indulgent papa, My dear
   You owe to indulgent papa.

**3.**
You surely can't say,
That you've not had your way —
In each of our family broils,
While I vow and declare,
You have had your full share,
In all of our National spoils.

*Chorus*:
   In all of our National spoils,
      Carrie dear,
   In all of our National spoils.

**4.**
Now be warned of your fate
Before it's too late,
Like a dear little innocent lamb,
Come out of your pet,
And do not forget,
All the kindness of good Uncle Sam.

*Chorus*:
   All the kindness of good Uncle Sam,
      Sister Carrie,
   All the kindness of good Uncle Sam.

**5.**
Some day all forlorn,
Bedraggled and torn,
Like the Prodigal Son in his need,
You will knock at the door,
And come home once more,
Nor venture again to Secede.

*Chorus*:
   Nor venture again to Secede,
      Sister Carrie,
   Nor venture again to Secede.

**6.**
The palmetto tree,
No shelter will be,
When the dark clouds of anarchy lower,
You will long for the rest,
Of our own Eagle's Nest,
And the Strong Arm of Federal Power.

*Chorus*:
   The strong Arm of Federal Power,
      Miss Carrie,
   The Strong Arm of Federal Power.

**7.**
Now dear little Sis,
Come give me a kiss,
To make up these Family Jars,
Secession shall never,
Our Union dissever,
Hurra! for the Stripes and the Stars;

*Chorus*:
   Hurra! for the Stripes and the Stars,
      Dear Carrie,
   Hurra! for the Stripes and the Stars.

# Uncle Sam, What Ails You?

Words: Charles C. Sawyer
Music: John M. Loretz

After the fall of Vicksburg and the surrender of Gettysburg, some Northerners envisaged an immediate end of the war. This song confirms Uncle Sam's strength and his efforts to continue the fight.

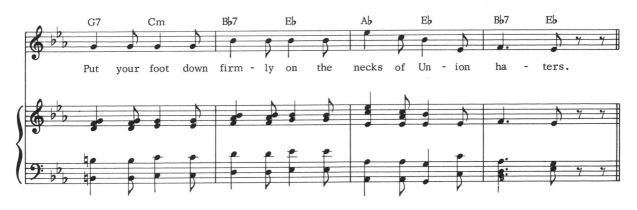

Put your foot down firm - ly on the necks of Un - ion ha - ters.

**Chorus**

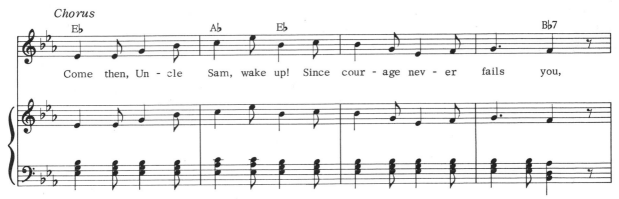

Come then, Un - cle Sam, wake up! Since cour - age nev - er fails you,

Crush all trai - tors, North or South! Un - cle Sam, what ails you? ails you?

2.
Confiscate their stocks and farms,
    Do it with a vigor,
If it will our Union save,
    Confiscate the ———
Confiscate all, everything,
    Even to their whiskey,
Till they find that to Rebel
    Is getting rather risky.

*Chorus*: Come then, etc.

3.
Uncle Sam, we know you're strong
    Both on land and water,
Why then with these Rebels play?
    Meet them as you ought'er!
Meet them with the sword and gun;
    Nor for a moment falter,
Meet them man to man, at least,
    Meet them with the halter!

*Chorus*: Come then, etc.

# Where Are You Going, Abe Lincoln?

Words: Anonymous
Music: "Lord Lovel"

The old English ballad of "Lord Lovel" was widely sung in the South. It is the story of unrequited love in which the lover dies a tragic death mourning the loss of his Lady Nancy.

In this Civil War version, the South satirizes Lincoln's expectations and encounters in a similar sequence. Lady "Lizzie Todd" is the heroine who probes and ponders the answers.

Moderately and expressively

1. Abe Lin-coln he stood at the White___ House gate A-comb-ing his milk white steed.___ A-long came his La-dy Liz-zie Todd A-wish-ing her lov-er good speed, speed, speed, A-wish-ing her lov-er good speed.___ A-wish-ing her lov-er good

speed, speed, speed, A - wish-ing her lov-er good speed._____ see._____

2.

"And where are you going, Abe Lincoln, " she said
"And where are you going, " said she.
"I am going to my dear Lady Lizzie Todd
Old Richmond for to see, see, see,
Old Richmond for to see."
(Repeat last two lines)

3.

He hadn't been gone more'n a week or two
Fair Dixie land to see
When back he came to the White House Gate
All tattered and torn was he, he, he,
All tattered and torn was he.
(Repeat last two lines)

4.

"I'm out of breath, " Abe Lincoln he said,
"I'm out of breath, " said he.
"The Rebels have killed my old Scott horse
And so I skedadled de, de, de,
And so I skedadled de, de.
(Repeat last two lines)

5.

"They tore my plaid and long tail blue,
And my long tail blue, " said he.
"My McClellan horse, I think will do
And I'll ride him around, " said he, he, he,
"And I'll ride him around, " said he.
(Repeat last two lines)

6.

He hadn't been gone more'n a month or two
Old Richmond for to see
When back he came to the White House Gate
His Lizzie Todd he must see, see, see,
His Lizzie Todd he must see.
(Repeat last two lines)

7.

"How do you flourish, Abe Lincoln, " she said
"How do you flourish, " said she.
"My coat I tore down on the Lee shore
Of chic o hom-inee - nee - nee
Of chic o hom-inee."
(Repeat last two lines)

8.

"You look so lank and lean, " she said
"You look so lank and lean."
"My horse fell on an old Stonewall
Down in the land of Dixie, ie, ie,
Down in the land of Dixie."
(Repeat last two lines)

9.

Then Abe Lincoln bestrode his Burnside horse,
But he "didged" at the Rebel fire,
And he threw the baboon heels over head
And there he stuck in the mire, ire, ire,
And there he stuck in the mire.
(Repeat last two lines)

# Jeff Davis' Dream

Words and Music:
Bernard Covert

Originally, the Zouaves were a tribe of "Kabyles" living among the Jurjua Mountains in Algeria. In more recent times this was the name of a body of infantry in the French service. They were known for their valor, dazzling costumes and spectacular drills. They wore gaiters or baggy red trousers, short open vests decorated with golden braids, and a colored tassled cap or turban. A number of Civil War regiments adopted this costume and thrilled their audiences with their startingly adroit drills.

In this song, the North expresses hope that President Davis will feel guilty for his treachery.

1. Jeff Da-vis a-woke one morn' from a dream, A hor-ri-ble dream, a hor-ri-ble dream; He jumped out of bed with a ter-ri-ble scream, A ter-ri-ble scream gave he.___ He dream'd that a mud-sill stood close by his bed, In the

garb of a Zou - ave in flan - nel red; With a noose made of hemp, slip-ping

o - ver his head, Say-ing come a - long trai-tor with me. _____ he. _____

2.

Jeff Davis he stared, he trembled and shook;
He was mightily scared and by friends all forsook;
For a very long passage he knew he was booked,
He knew he was booked did he.
He stood all aghast, as he viewed a strange scrawl,
It was the handwriting he had seen on the wall,
Predicting at once secession's downfall.
What a mighty great fall, said he.

3.

Dear Yancey, Cobb, Benjamin, Thompson and Floyd;
Your hearts are as pure as the gold unalloyed;
But I verily fear we shall all be destroyed,
And I'm greatly annoyed said he.
Of our villainous doings I know you won't peach;
For thirty long years secession we've preached.
And we never stole anything out of our reach.
Quite out of our reach, said he.

4.

Old England and France, their gold did advance,
For tobacco and cotton they wanted a chance,
To break the blockade they promised their aid,
They were not afraid not they.
But the Yankees by magic they sent down a fleet,
And closed all our rivers and harbors complete
And caused us too often to beat a retreat,
And suffer defeat, said he.

5.

Our northern secessioners made us believe
They'd be with us, fight with us, never deceive,
But their cowardly hearts have caused us to grieve,
Have caused us to grieve, said he.
Both England and France they now look askance
To aid us they've not even broken a lance
Those big bullies have left us on nothing to dance,
On nothing to dance, said he.

6.

Ye fools of ambition take heed of my fate;
Once proud my position of power and estate;
Had I remained loyal, I might still have been great
I deserve the world's hate, said he.
My countrymen all, take warning by me;
Stand by the old flag and true liberty
Prosperous, glorious and honored, you'll be,
In spite of the world, said he.

# Treasury Rats

Words and Music:
Anonymous

War is an expensive venture.  The total cost for the North was about $5,000,000,000 and for the South, about $3,000,000,000.  The Secretary of the Treasury, Salmon P. Chase, was confronted with an empty treasury in 1861 when Lincoln issued his first call for volunteers.  Storms of protest, satire and ridicule accompanied the Government's contemplated use of paper money.  Here is a rollicking patter ditty attacking usurers, "note shavers," manipulators, "squandering speculators," and copperheads.

Quickly with animation

1. Trea-su-ry rats are swarm-ing a-round, Ev-'ry-where o - ver and un-der the ground, In

all the hou-ses and all the shops, From cel-lar floors to gar - ret tops, Oh,

con - found the Trea-su-ry Rats! They laugh to scorn all traps and snares, They

run up the walls and down the stairs, O-ver the beds and through the floors,

gnaw great holes in pan-try doors. Greed-y, dirt-y, lank and lean, Their

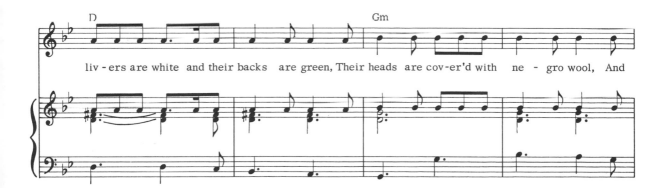

liv-ers are white and their backs are green, Their heads are cov-er'd with ne-gro wool, And

*Refrain*

bel-lies they have that are nev-er full. Oh, con-found the Trea-su-ry Rats!

### 2.

Rats are hungry enough!
Tr̶e on earth can be too tough,
N̶o̶ too hard, or soft, or sweet,
N̶vy, or light, for them to eat.
*̶orus*:
̶n, Confound the Treasury Rats!
̶ddy for blankets, coats and hats,
̶just the thing for Treasury Rats;
̶er ironclads they lick their lips,
And countless fleets of rotten ships.
Ammunition, shot, and shell,
Horses in numbers none can tell,
Cannon and rifles, powder and ball,
These ravenous vermin gobble them all, -
*Chorus*:
Oh, Confound the Treasury Rats!

### 3.

Treasury Rats have friends at court,
Chasing them therefore is ticklish sport;
They all are "loyal," — every Rat, —
A "traitor" you are if you question that! —
*Chorus*:
Oh, Confound the Treasury Rats!
Go to Washington, clap your ear
To the Treasury Vault, and there'll you hear,
Every moment of night and day,
Ten thousand Rats all gnawing away!
Hundreds of presses, at high steam power,
Print the "money" these Rats devour,
And if "Copperheads" try to scare them away,
"Hush!" — the Government papers say, —
*Chorus*:
Oh, Confound the Treasury Rats!

### 4.

Down on the battle field I stood,
Where brethren had shed each other's blood;
And armies of Rats were moving round,
Hither and thither over the ground;
*Chorus*:
Oh, Confound the Treasury Rats!
I looked and I saw their snouts were red,
As they gorged themselves from off the dead;
They stroked their whiskers, and switched their tails,
And danced for joy in the tainted gales!
They tore the flesh from the dead men's bones,
And chattered and squealed, 'mid the wounded's groans,
"Sure 'tis a nation's noblest bliss
To keep us Rats in victuals like this!"
*Chorus*:
Oh, Confound the Treasury Rats!

### 5.

Treasury Rats now rule the land!
Everything moves by their command;
They cut out the work, and handle the pay,
And a charming song they sing today.
*Chorus*:
Oh, Confound the Treasury Rats!
"Traitors and Copperheads, penniless knaves,
"You are the stuff to fill soldiers' graves!
"The country's great and only need
"Is that we shall make money, while you shall bleed!
This is true "loyalty!" — on with the war!
And this is what you are fighting it for!
Go on killing each other — gloriously —
Till we are as rich as we'd like to be!"
*Chorus*:
Oh, Confound the Treasury Rats!

### 6.

Coming events cast shadows before!
The reign of the Rats will soon be o'er;
Some already have left the ship,
And others will soon be giving the slip,—
*Chorus*:
Oh, Confound the Treasury Rats!
Water they hate, and water they fear,
And water will soon be everywhere;
From West and East and South and North
Rivers of wrath are rolling forth.
Tides are rising, mighty in power,
Higher and higher, hour by hour,
And, when November has come for good,
With one, vast overwhelming flood,—
*Chorus*:
We'll drown out the Treasury Rats!

# Portraits

# Farewell Father, Friend and Guardian

Words: L. M. Dawn
Music: George F. Root

The tragic assassination of President Lincoln on April fourteenth shocked the nation and the world. Numerous songs expressed feelings of grief, sorrow and sympathy. This is the most famous of them all. The repeated rhythmic figure, which reminds us of those somber drum beats, supports the noble hymn-like melody.

hand;  Tho' pre-serv'd  his dear-est  trea-sure,  Our re-deem'd  be-lov-ed  land.

*Chorus*

Fare-well  fath-er,  friend and guard-ian,  Thou hast join'd  the mar-tyr band,  But thy

glor-ious work re-main-eth,  Our re-deem'd  be-lov-ed  land.  land.

2.

Thro' our night of bloody struggle,
Ever dauntless, firm and true,
Bravely, gently forth he led us,
Till the morn burst on our view —
Till he saw the day of triumph,
Saw the field our heroes won;
Then his honor'd life was ended,
Then his glorious work was done.

*Chorus*: Farewell Father, etc.

3.

When from mountain, hill and valley,
To their homes our brave boys come,
When with welcome notes we greet them,
Song and cheer, and pealing drum;
When we miss our lov'd ones fallen,
When to weep we turn aside;
Then for him our tears shall mingle —
He has suffer'd — he has died.

*Chorus*:  Farewell Father, etc.

4.

Honor'd leader, long and fondly
Shall by mem'ry cherish'd be;
Hearts shall bless thee for their freedom,
Hearts unborn shall sigh for thee;
He who gave thee might and wisdom,
Gave thy spirit sweet release;
Farewell, father, friend and guardian,
Rest forever, rest in peace.

*Chorus*:  Farewell Father, etc.

# Sherman the Brave

Words: Charles Haynes
Music: J. E. Haynes

Numerous songs left an imperishable record of the famed General Sherman. "Marching Through Georgia" and "Hold The Fort" (included in another section of this book) were among the most popular songs of the war. This is a patriotic song which sings praise for his bravery and courage in the cause of freedom.

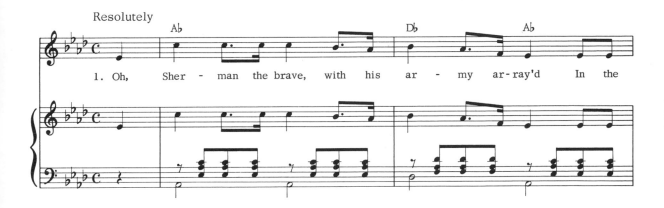

1. Oh, Sher - man the brave, with his ar - my ar - ray'd In the

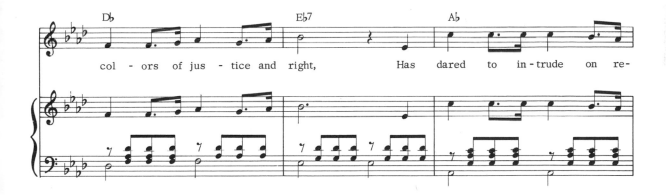

col - ors of jus - tice and right, Has dared to in - trude on re-

bel - lions false ground, And put the fierce trai - tors to flight. Un-

76

mind - ful of hard - ships, e - lat - ed with hope, At the

pros - pect of glo - rious re - nown, Our sol - diers pressed on at the

dawn of the day, And soon was the great bat - tle won.

*Chorus*

Then hail to brave Sher - man so no - ble and true, Let

all sound his prais - es a - far, He's passed thro' the con - flict un-

harmed by the foe, We'll wel-come our na - tion's bright star. star.

**2.**

And still step by step, he right onward doth press,
And yet foot by foot doth restore
The dark tainted land, which by treason's foul hand
From the Union was cruelly torn;
Till on Sumter's proud height with courage and might
In triumph again he doth wave
Our glorious flag, which just four years ago,
Was trailed in the dust of the slave.

*Chorus*: Then hail to brave Sherman, etc.

**3.**

Then cheer for brave Sherman, defender of right,
Who led forth our patriot band,
He's won the bright laurels; his glory shines forth;
Let all sound his praise through the land.
Yet here 'twill not end — when long years have roll'd on
And low in the dust he doth lie
Will the mem'ry of him, "Gen'l Sherman the brave,"
In the people's proud hearts never die.

*Chorus*: Then hail to brave Sherman, etc.

# The Sword of Robert E. Lee

Words: Father Abram J. Ryan
Music: A. E. Blackmar

The Civil War has left us with vivid impressions of our national heroes. Lee astride "Traveller" has become folklore and legend. This song is the most famous setting to the poem by Ryan, who was the "poet-priest of the Confederacy." The song intones the dignity and noble character of the General who even in defeat was respected by all.

1. Forth from its scab-bard,____ pure and __ bright, Forth flash'd the sword of

Lee! Forth from its scab-bard,____ pure and__ bright,

Forth flash'd the sword of Lee! Far in the front

of the dead-ly fight, High o'er the brave, in the cause___ of the Right,

Its stain-less sheen_____ like a bea-con light, Led us to vic-to-

ry. Sword! sword of brave Rob - ert Lee! Sword!

sword of brave Rob - ert Lee!_____ ly.

2.

Out of its scabbard, where full long
   It slumber'd peacefully,
Out of its scabbard, where full long
   It slumber'd peacefully,
Rous'd from its rest by the great battle song.
Shielding the feeble, smiting the strong,
Guarding the right, avenging the wrong,
   Gleamed the sword of Lee!

*Chorus*: Sword! sword, etc.

3.

Forth from its scabbard, high in the air,
   Beneath Virginia's sky,
Forth from its scabbard, high in the air,
   Beneath Virginia's sky,
And they who saw it gleaming there,
And knew who bore it, knelt to swear,
That where that sword led, they would dare
   To follow and to die.

*Chorus*: Sword! sword, etc.

4.

Out of its scabbard, never hand
   Waved sword from stain as free,
Out of its scabbard, never hand
   Waved sword from stain as free,
Nor purer sword led braver band,
Nor braver bled for a brighter land,
Nor brighter land had cause as grand,
   Nor cause, a chief like Lee.

*Chorus*: Sword! sword, etc.

5.

Forth from its scabbard, how we prayed
   That sword might victor be!
Forth from its scabbard, how we prayed
   That sword might victor be.
And when our triumph was delayed,
And many a heart grew sore afraid,
We still hoped on, while gleamed the blade
   Of noble Robert Lee.

*Chorus*: Sword! sword, etc.

6.

Forth from its scabbard, all in vain,
   Forth flashed the sword of Lee,
Forth from its scabbard, all in vain,
   Forth flashed the sword of Lee.
'Tis shrouded now in its sheath again,
It sleeps the sleep of our noble slain,
Defeated, yet without a stain,
   Proudly and peacefully.

*Chorus*: Sword! sword, etc.

# Honor to Sheridan

Words: Paulina
Music: George F. Root

Philip Henry Sheridan was the famed cavalry officer of the Union Armies. He won distinction for his daring and brilliant charge up Missionary Ridge. General Grant placed him in charge of his cavalry and in this post he proved himself the most able leader of the Union Army. An anonymous "rhymer" of the period put it:

"Phil Sheridan down in the valley made
A ride the "rebs" to often:
'Twas "Out with the blade
Away with the spade;
Fight early, and fight often!"

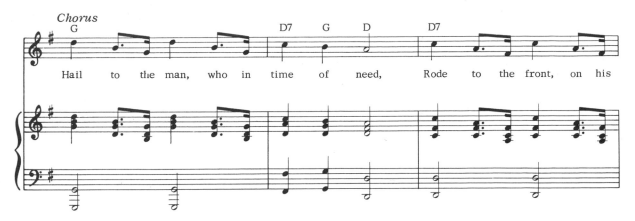

Chorus

Hail to the man, who in time of need, Rode to the front, on his

coal black steed! Hail to the man in the na-tion's van! Hon - or for-ev - er to

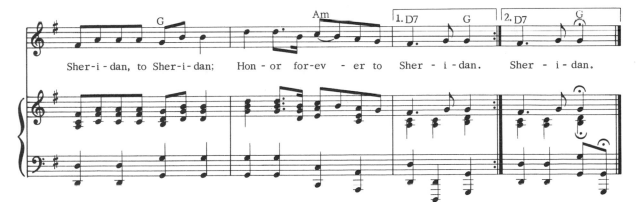

Sher-i-dan, to Sher-i-dan; Hon - or for-ev - er to Sher - i - dan. Sher - i - dan.

2.

Oh, the grateful land hath a warm right hand,
In the welcome her own hath won her;
For the tried and true — for the "Boy in Blue"
That our souls all delight to honor.

*Chorus*: Hail to the man, etc.

3.

As we dwell with pride, on his battle ride,
Let us speak of his civic glory;
Let the joybells ring, and the banners fling
To the winds, with the hero's story.

*Chorus*: Hail to the man, etc.

# Stonewall Jackson's Way

Words: John W. Palmer
Music: Anonymous

This poem was written during the battle at Antietam by John Palmer, a physician, poet, playwright and newspaper correspondent. It is reported that the original copy was lost, and later found on the body of a Confederate sergeant of Stonewall's Brigade who was killed at Winchester. * The song describes Jackson, the devout Christian, and the spirit of his men.

*Heaps, W. & P., *The Singing Sixties*
University of Oklahoma Press

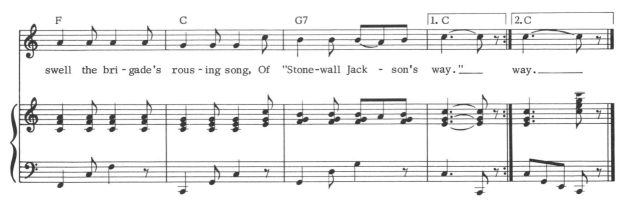

swell the bri-gade's rous-ing song, Of "Stone-wall Jack - son's way." way.

**2.**

We see him now — the old slouched hat
Couched o'er his eye askew —
The shrewd, dry smile — the speech so pat,
So calm, so blunt, so true;
The "Blue Light Elder" knows 'em well:
Says he, "That's Banks, he's fond of shell;
Lord, save his soul! we'll give him — " well
That's "Stonewall Jackson's way."

**3.**

Silence! Ground arms! Kneel all! Caps off!
Old "Blue Light's" going to pray;
Strangle the fool that dares to scoff!
Attention! It's his way!
Appealing from his native sod,
"Hear us, Almighty God!
Lay bare thine arm, stretch forth thy rod,
Amen!" That's Stonewall Jackson's way.

**4.**

He's in the saddle now! Fall in!
Steady! The whole brigade!
Hill's at the ford, cut off; we'll win
His way out, ball and blade.
What matter if our shoes are worn?
What matter if our feet are torn?
Quick step! we're with him ere the dawn!
That's Stonewall Jackson's way!

**5.**

The sun's bright lances rout the mists
Of morning — and, by George!
Here's Longstreet, struggling in the lists,
Hemmed in an ugly gorge.
Pope and his Yankees, whipped before;
"Bayonetts and grape!" hear Stonewall roar.
"Charge, Stuart! pay off Ashby's score,"
Is Stonewall Jackson's way!

**6.**

Ah! maiden, wait, and watch, and yearn,
For news of Stonewall's band!
Ah! widow, read — with eyes that burn —
That ring upon thy hand!
Ah! wife, sew on, hope on, and pray!
That life shall not be all forlorn —
The foe had better ne'er been born,
That gets in Stonewall's way.

# Beauregard

Words: F. E. D.
Music: H. D.

Both sides idolized their military heroes. The South Carolinians called Beauregard "Old Bory," and the *Examiner* hailed him as "Beauregard Felix." Among the Romans, this term signified "happy, fortunate, and favored of the gods." In this song, the hero of the "First Bull Run" is extolled for leading the fight for freedom.

steady hands strike blow for blow, With our Beau - re - gard! Beau - re - gard! Beau - re - gard! Beau - re - gard! Beau - re - gard! Beau - re - gard.

2.

Shall a nation plead in vain?
  Beauregard! Beauregard!
Patriots ne'er the cause disdain,
  Beauregard! Beauregard!
Our father's smiles presage success
  In our war;
Our mothers' prayers our cause will bless,
  Under Beauregard, etc.

3.

Remember well Manassas' field!
  Beauregard! Beauregard!
Ever thus make tyrants yield,
  Beauregard! Beauregard!
With armor bright in glorious fight
  The victor's star
Fell in never-fading light
  Upon our Beauregard, etc.

# O, I'm a Good Old Rebel

Words: Anonymous
Music: Wild Western Melody of "Joe Bowers"

It was not easy for some Confederates to "forgive and forget." While the victor extended a welcoming hand, the defeated often retained feelings of a stubborn and acrid kind. In this song the "old timer" still clings to his ideas and "won't be reconstructed."

This song was "respectfully dedicated" to the Honorable Thad. Stevens.

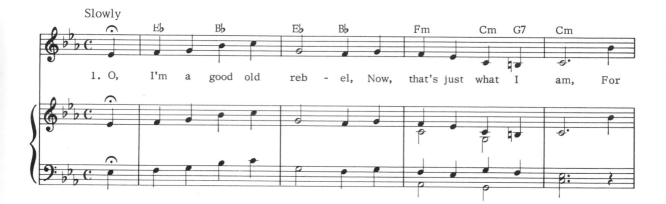

1. O, I'm a good old reb - el, Now, that's just what I am, For

this "Fair Land of Free - dom" I do not care at all; I'm

glad I fit a - gainst it, I on - ly wish we'd won; And

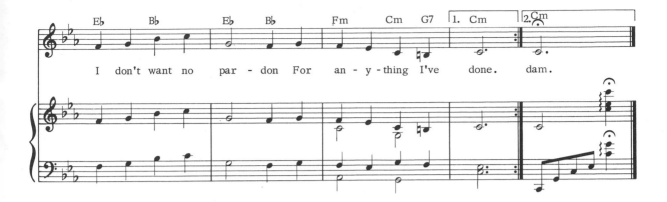

I don't want no par - don For an - y -thing I've done. dam.

2.
I hates the Constitution,
    This Great Republic, too,
I hates the Freedman's Buro,
    In uniforms of blue;
I hates the nasty eagle,
    With all his brags and fuss,
The lyin', thievin' Yankees,
    I hates 'em wuss and wuss.

3.
I hates the Yankee nation
    And everything they do,
I hates the Declaration
    Of Independence, too;
I hates the glorious Union —
    'Tis dripping with our blood —
I hates their striped banner,
    I fit it all I could.

4.
I followed old Mas' Robert
    For four year, near about,
Got wounded in three places
    And starved at Pint Lookout;
I cotch the moomatism
    A campin' in the snow,
But I killed a chance o' Yankees,
    I'd like to kill some mo'.

5.
Three hundred thousand Yankees
    Is stiff in Southern dust;
We got three hundred thousand
    Before they conquered us;
They died of Southern fever
    And Southern steel and shot,
I wish they was three million
    Instead of what we got.

6.
I can't take up my musket
    And fight 'em now no more,
But I aint a going to love 'em,
    Now that is sarten sure;
And I don't want no pardon
    For what I was and am,
I won't be reconstructed
    And I don't care a dam.

# Riding a Raid
## (A Tribute to J.E.B. Stuart)

Words: Anonymous
Music: "The Bonnie Dundee"

They called him "Jeb Stuart" and "Beauty Stuart." The famed cavalry officer James Ewell Brown Stuart was handsome in appearance and daring in his raids. A member of his staff, J. E. Cooke, wrote:

> "this gay bearing of the man was plainly unaffected and few persons could resist its influence. At Culpepper the infantry were electrified by the laughter and singing of Stuart as he led them in the charge, and at Chancellorsville where he commanded Jackson's corps."*

After a daring raid with bullets whizzing all around, he said to G. C. Eggleston—"Did you ever time this horse for a half mile?"**

1. 'Tis old Stone - wall the Reb - el that leans on his sword, And while we are mount-ing prays low to the Lord: "Now_ each cav - a - lier that loves hon - or and right, Let him fol - low the feath - er of Stu - art to-night." Come

*Cooke, J. E., *Personal Portraits*—1871
**Botkin, B., *Civil War Treasury*

tight-en your girth and slack-en your rein; Come buck-le your blan-ket and

hol-ster a-gain; Try the click of your trig-ger and bal-ance your blade, For

he must ride sure that goes rid-ing a raid! rid-ing a raid.

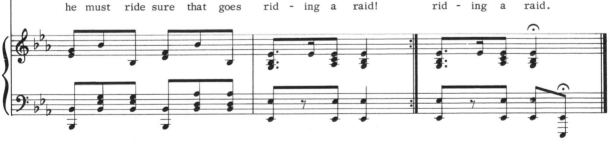

2.

Now gallop, now gallop to swim or to ford!
Old Stonewall, still watching, prays low to the Lord:
"Good Bye dear old Rebel! the river's not wide,
And Maryland's lights in her window to guide."
Come tighten your girth and slacken your rein;
Come buckle your blanket and holster again;
Try the click of your trigger and balance your blade
For he must ride sure that goes Riding a Raid!

3.

There's a man in a white house with blood on his mouth!
If there's knaves in the North, there are braves in the South.
We are three thousand horses, and not one afraid;
We are three thousand sabres and not a dull blade.
Come tighten your girth and slacken your rein;
Come buckle your blanket and holster again.
Try the click of your trigger and balance your blade.
For he must ride sure that goes Riding a Raid.

4.

Then gallop, then gallop by ravines and rocks!
Who would bar us the way take his toll in hard knocks;
For with these points of steel, on the line of Penn
We have made some fine strokes - and we'll make 'em again.
Then tighten your girth and slacken your rein;
Come buckle your blanket and holster again;
Try the click of your trigger and balance your blade,
For he must ride sure, that goes Riding a Raid.

# Kingdom Coming
## (Year of Jubilo)

Words and Music:
Henry Clay Work

The composer was an active abolitionist and one of the most popular song writers of the North. This lively and amusing song shows the influence of the "Minstrel Stage" and was composed before anti-slavery became a "hot issue." The author places a Negro in the position of watching "de massa" flee before the advancing Union Armies.

1. Say, dar-keys, hab you seen de mas-sa, Wid de muff-stash on his face, Go long de road some time dis morn-in', Like he gwine to leab de place? He seen a smoke, way up de rib-ber, Whar de Link-um gum-boats lay; He

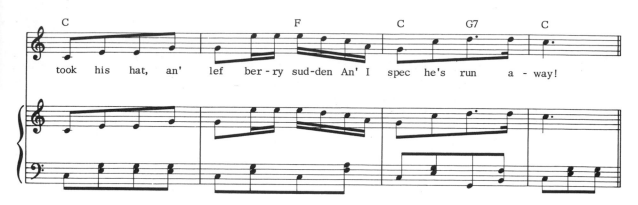

took his hat, an' lef ber-ry sud-den An' I spec he's run a - way!

*Chorus*

De mas - sa run? ha, ha! De dar - key stay? ho, ho! It

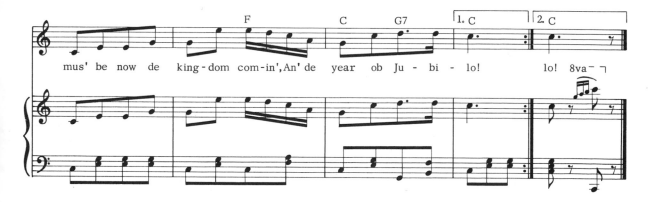

mus' be now de king-dom com-in',An' de year ob Ju - bi - lo! lo! 8va

2.

He six foot one way, two feet tudder,
　　An' he weigh tree hundred pound,
His coat so big, he couldn't pay de tailor,
　　An' it won't go half way round.
He drill so much dey call him Cap'an,
　　An' he get so drefful tann'd,
I spec he try an' fool dem Yankees
　　For to tink he's contraband.

*Chorus*: De massa run? ha, ha! etc.

3.

De darkeys feel so lonesome libing
   In de log-house on de lawn,
Dey move dar tings to massa's parlor
   For to keep it while he's gone.
Dar's wine an' cider in de kitchen,
   An' de darkeys dey'll hab some;
I spose dey'll all be cornfiscated
   When de Linkum sojers come.

*Chorus*: De massa run? ha, ha! etc.

4.

De oberseer he make us trouble,
   An' he dribe us round a spell;
We lock him up in de smokehouse cellar,
   Wid de key trown in de well.
De whip is lost, de han'cuff broken,
   But de massa'll hab his pay;
He's ole enough, big enough, ought to known better
   Dan to went an' run away.

*Chorus*: De massa run? ha, ha! etc.

# Wake Nicodemus

Words and Music:
Henry Clay Work

This is regarded as one of the most beautiful songs of the period. In hymn-like tones, the slave humbly prays for the day of Jubilee. His plaintive cry, "Wake me up," reflects the ardent hopes of the Negro.

In slow, firm tempo

1. Nic - o - de - mus, the slave, was of Af - ri - can birth, And was bought for a bag - ful of gold; He was reck - on'd as part of the salt of the earth, But he died years a - go ver - y old. 'Twas his

last sad re-quest, so we laid him a-way In the trunk of an old hol-low

tree. "Wake me up!" was his charge, "at the first break of day, Wake me

up for the great Ju-bi-lee!" *Chorus* The "Good Time com-ing" is

al-most here! It was long, long, long on the way! Now,

run and tell E-li-ja to hur-ry up Pomp, And meet us at the gum-tree down in the swamp, To wake Nic-o-de-mus to-day. day.

**2.**

He was known as a prophet — at least was as wise —
   For he told of the battles to come;
And he trembled with dread when he roll'd up his eyes,
   And we heeded the shake of his thumb.
Though he clothed us with fear, yet the garments he wore
   Were in patches at elbow and knee;
And he still wears the suit that he used to of yore,
   As he sleeps in the old hollow tree.

*Chorus*:   The "Good time Coming," etc.

**3.**

Nicodemus was never the sport of the lash,
   Though the bullet has oft crossed his path;
There were none of his masters so brave or so rash,
   As to face such a man in his wrath.
Yet his great heart with kindness was filled to the brim —
   He obeyed who was born to command:
But he long'd for the morning which then was so dim —
   The morning which now is at hand.

*Chorus*:   The "Good time Coming," etc.

**4.**

'Twas a long weary night — we were almost in fear
   That the future was more than he knew;
'Twas a long weary night — but the morning is near,
   And the words of our prophet are true.
There are signs in the sky that the darkness is gone —
   There are tokens in endless array;
When the storm which had seemingly banished the dawn,
   Only hastens the advent of day.

*Chorus*:   The "Good time Coming," etc.

## Part Two

# *Volunteering and Conscription*

# *Army Life In Camp*

# Volunteering
# and
# Conscription

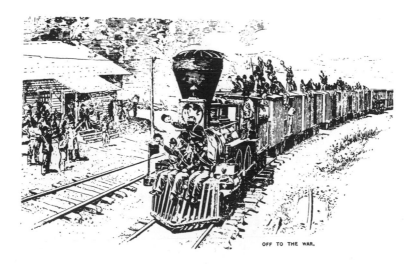

OFF TO THE WAR.

# Abraham's Daughter
## or
## The Raw Recruit

Words and Music:
Septimus Winner

Both North and South employed the volunteer and conscription systems. At the beginning of the War, patriotism was running high in both sections. The response was so great, that neither government had sufficient arms and equipment for all. Soon, some who had had a taste of war failed to re-enlist at the expiration of their term of service. Others sensed opportunities for high wages or large profits at home and displayed no eagerness to shoulder a musket. With such a state of affairs, both sections resorted to bounties to stimulate enlistments. In July, 1861, the Federal Government initiated the practice of offering $100 to every volunteer, which was shortly increased to $302 for recruits and $402 for veterans.

This jovial ditty is about a volunteer from New York City's Fire Department and was one of the most popular songs of the war.

1. Oh!__ kind folks list-en to my song, It is no i-dle sto-ry, It's__ all a-bout a vol-un-teer Who's goin' to fight__ for__ glo-ry; Now don't you think that I am right? For I am noth-ing short-er. And__

I be-long to the Fire Zou, Zous, And don't you think I ought-er, We're go-in' down to Wash-ing-ton To fight for A-bra-ham's daugh-ter. daugh-ter.

**2.**

Oh! should you ask me who she am,
   Columbia is her name, sir,
She is the child of Abraham
   Or Uncle Sam, the same, sir.
Now if I fight, why aint I right?
   And don't you think I oughter.
The volunteers are a pouring in
   From ev'ry loyal quarter,
And I'm goin' long to Washington
   To fight for Abraham's daughter.

**3.**

They say we have no officers,
   But ah! they are mistaken;
And soon you'll see the rebels run.
   With all the fuss they're makin';
For there is one who just sprung up,
   He'll show the foe no quarter,
(McClellan is the man I mean,)
   You know he hadn't oughter,
For he's gone down to Washington
   To fight for Abraham's daughter.

**4.**

We'll have a spree with Johnny Bull,
   Perhaps, some day or other,
And won't he have his fingers full,
   If not a deal of bother;
For Yankee boys are just the lads
   Upon the land or water;
And won't we have a "bully" fight,
   And don't you think we oughter,
If he is caught at any time,
   Insulting Abraham's daughter.

**5.**

But let us lay all jokes aside,
   It is a sorry question;
The man who would these States divide
   Should hang for his suggestion.
One Country and one Flag, I say,
   Whoe'er the war may slaughter;
So I'm goin' as a Fire Zou-a,
   And don't you think I oughter,
I'm going down to Washington
   To fight for Abraham's daughter.

# Johnny is Gone for a Soldier

Words: Septimus Winner
Music: Old Irish folk song

Alan Lomax, in his *Folk Songs of North America,* claims that this song dates "from the period after the Treaty of Limerick," when "like a flight of wild geese. . . .many young Irish patriots fled to France and served in the armies of the French king." In the old Irish version, the girl dyes her petticoat red to show that she is engaged and loyal to her absent Johnny. In this American setting she does likewise, but for a more sorrowful reason. The meaning of the Irish "shule Agrah" is "Come with me my love."* The English spelling is used here—"Shool-Agrah."

1. I trace these gar-dens o'er_ and_ o'er, Med-i-tate on each sweet flow'r,

Think-ing of each hap-py_ hour, Oh, John-ny is gone for a sol-dier.

*Chorus*

Shool-a Shool-a Shool-a-grah, Time can on-ly heal my woe,

*Lomax, Alan, *The Folk Songs of North America,* p. 34
Doubleday & Co.

Since the lad of my heart from me did go, Oh, John-ny is gone for a sol-dier. sol-dier.

**2.**
Some say my love is gone to France,
There his fortune to advance,
And if I find him it's but a chance,
Oh! Johnny is gone for a Soldier.

*Chorus*: Shool-a, Shool-a, etc.

**3.**
I'll sell my frock, I'll sell my wheel,
I'll buy my love a sword of steel,
So in the battle he may reel,
Oh, Johnny is gone for a Soldier.

*Chorus*: Shool-a, Shool-a, etc.

**4.**
I wish I was on yonder hill,
It's there I'd sit and cry my fill,
So ev'ry tear might turn a mill,
Oh, Johnny is gone for a Soldier.

*Chorus*: Shool-a, Shool-a, etc.

**5.**
I'll dye my dress all over red,
And o'er the world I'll beg my bread,
So all my friends may think me dead,
Oh, Johnny is gone for a Soldier.

*Chorus*: Shool-a, Shool-a, etc.

# You Are Going to the Wars, Willie Boy!

Words and Music:
John Hill Hewitt

This song combines the sentiments of "Southern Chivalry" and spirited patriotism. While "Willie Boy" will be "fighting for the right," his glittering new uniform and "shining buttons too" may win the hearts of other pretty girls.

2.

You'll be fighting for the right,
   Willie boy, Willie boy,
You'll be fighting for the right and your home;
And you'll strike the blow with might,
   Willie boy, Willie boy,
'Mid the thundering of cannon and of drum;
With an arm as true as steel,
   You'll make the foemen feel
The vengence of a Southerner,
   Too proud to cringe or kneel.
Oh! should you fall in strife,
   Willie boy, Willie boy,
Oh, should you fall in strife on the plain,
I'll pine away my life,
   Willie boy, Willie boy,
And never, never wear a smile again.

# The Young Volunteer

**Words and Music:**
John H. Hewitt

The young Southern soldier marches off to war with this spirited march-like tune. He takes his vows for country and flag and for the girls he left behind. The author attended West Point with Beauregard, Lee and Polk. He was one of the most prolific song writers of the South.

With force, but not fast

1. Our flag is un-furl'd, and our arms flash bright, As the sun wades up the sky; But ere I ___ join the ___ doubt - ful fight, Love - ly maid, I would say "Good - bye," I'm a

young\_\_\_ vol - un - teer, and my heart is true To our flag that woos the

wind; Then three cheers\_ for that flag and our coun - try too, And the

*Chorus*

girls we leave be - hind. Then a - dieu,\_\_\_ then a - dieu, 'tis the

last\_\_\_ bu - gle's strain That is fall - ing on the ear; Should it

so— be de-creed that we ne'er meet a-gain, Oh, re-mem-ber the Young Vol-un - teer.

2.

When over the desert, thro' burning rays,
    With a heavy heart I tread;
Or when I breast the cannon's blaze,
    And bemoan my comrades dead,
Then, then I will think of my home and you,
    And our flag shall kiss the wind;
With huzza for our cause and our country too,
    And the girls we leave behind.

*Chorus:*    Then adieu, then adieu, etc.

# Take Your Gun and Go, John

Words and Music:
H. T. Merrill

This loving and patriotic wife of a Union volunteer assures her husband that she will take care of the children and keep the home fires burning. Above all she pleads that he take a pair of blankets which she wove and spun as a girl—which will keep him warm "because they're made by me."

all our lit-tle stores, John; Yes leave them all to me.

**Chorus**

Then take your gun and go, Yes, take your gun and go, For

Ruth can drive the ox-en, John, And I can use the hoe. way.

2.
I've heard my grandsire tell, John,
    He fought at Bunker Hill,
He counted all his life and wealth
    His country's off'ring still.
Would I shame the brave old blood, John;
    That flow'd on Monmouth plain?
No! take your gun and go, John;
    Tho' I ne'er see you again.

*Chorus:* Then take your gun, etc.

**3.**

The army's short of blankets, John,
    Then take this heavy pair,
I spun and wove them when a girl,
    And work'd them with great care.
A rose in every corner, John;
    And here's my name, you see!
On the cold ground they'll warmer feel,
    Because they're made by me.

*Chorus*:  Then take your gun, etc.

**4.**

And, John, if God has willed it so
    We ne'er shall meet again,
I'll do the best for the children, John,
    In sorrow, want or pain.
On winter nights I'll teach them, John,
    All that I learned at school;
To love our country, keep her laws
    Obey the Savior's rule.

*Chorus*:  Then take your gun, etc.

**5.**

And now good-bye to you, John;
    I cannot say Farewell!
We'll hope and pray for the best, John;
    His goodness none can tell,
May His arm be round about you, John,
    To guard you night and day;
Be our beloved country's shield,
    Till war shall pass away.

*Chorus*:  Then take your gun, etc.

# Corporal Schnapps

Words and Music:
Henry Clay Work

This famous song writer of the North could not resist the temptation to try his hand at a comic song in dialect. The Minstrel Show at the time exerted a strong influence. A German born soldier complains about the "hard tack" in the army. But when he gets to the South, there is plenty of good sauerkraut and lager beer.

Not too fast

1. Mine heart ish pro-ken in-to lit-tle pits, I tells you friend what for;_____ Mine

schweet-heart, von coot pa-tri-o-tic kirl, She trives me off mit der war. I

fights for her der pat-tles of te flag, I schtrikes so prave as I can; Put

now long time she nix re-mem-pers me, And coes mit an-oth-er man.

*Chorus*

Ah! Mein frau-lein! You ish so fer-ry un — kind! You

coes mit Hans to Zher-man-y to live, And leaves poor Schnapps pe —

hind,_____ Leaves poor Schnapps pe - hind. free.

### 2.

I march all tay, no matter if der schtorm
 Pe worse ash Moses' flood;
I lays all night, mine head upon a schtump,
 And "sinks to schleep" in der mud.
Der nightmare comes — I catch him ferry pad —
 I treams I schleeps mit der Ghost;
I wakes next morning frozen in der cround,
 So schtiff as von schtone post.

*Chorus*: Ah! mein fraulein! etc.

### 3.

They kives me hartpread, tougher as a rock —
 It almost preaks mine zhaw;
I schplits him sometimes mit an iron wedge,
 And cuts him up mit a saw.
They kives me peef, so ferry, ferry salt,
 Like Sodom's wife, you know;
I surely dinks they put him in der prine
 Von huntred year aco.

*Chorus*: Ah! mein fraulein! etc.

### 4.

Py'n py we takes von city in der South —
 We schtays there von whole year;
I kits me sourcrout much as I can eat,
 Und blenty loccar pier.
I meets von laty repel in der schtreet,
 So handsome effer I see:
I makes to her von ferry callant pow —
 Put ah! she schpits on me.

*Chorus*: Ah! mein fraulein! etc.

### 5.

"Hart times!" you say, "what for you folunteer?"
 I told you, friend, what for:
Mine schweet-heart, von coot patriotic kirl,
 She trove me off mit der war.
Alas! Alas! mine bretty little von
 Vill schmile no more on me;
Put schtill I fights de pattles of te flag
 To set mine countries free.

*Chorus*: Ah! mein fraulein! etc.

# I Goes to Fight mit Sigel

Words: F. Poole
Music: Samuel Lover

Many soldiers of foreign birth fought valiantly and distinguished themselves in the Union Armies; there were a number of complete regiments made up of foreign born. General Franz Sigel, a German émigré, commanded the 2nd Missouri Brigade, fought at Pea Ridge, and went with Pope to Virginia. *

.This comic song in German dialect was very much favored by the Minstrel impersonators. The German born soldier evidently knows his American history, the cause for which he is fighting, and the heroism of the admired General.

*Commager, H. S., *The Blue and The Gray*, Vol. 1, P. 385
Bobbs Merrill Co.

save the Yan - kee Ea - gle; Un— now I— gets my

so - jer clothes; I'm go-ing to— fight mit Si - gel. Si - gel.

### 2.
Ven I comes from der Deutsche Countree
I vorks somedimes at baking;
Den I keeps a lager beer saloon,
Und den I goes shoe-making;
But now I was a sojer been
To save der Yankee Eagle,
To schlauch dem tam secession volks,
I goes to fight mit Sigel.

### 3.
I gets ein tam big rifle guns,
Und puts him to mine shoulder,
Den march so bold like a big jackhorse,
Und may been someding bolder;
I goes off mit de volunteers
To save der Yankee Eagle;
To give dem Rebel vellers fits.
I goes to fight mit Sigel.

### 4.
Dem Deutschen mens mit Sigel's band
At fighting have no rival;
Und ven Cheff Davis mens ve meet,
Ve schlauch em like de tuyvil.
Dere's only von ting vot I fear,
Ven pattling for der Eagle,
I vont get not no lager beer,
Ven I goes to fight mit Sigel.

### 5.
For rations dey gives salty pork,
I dinks dat was a great sell;
I petter likes de sauerkraut,
Der Schvitzer-kase und bretzel.
If Fighting Joe will give us dem,
Ve'll save der Yankee Eagle,
Und I'll put mine vrou in breech-a-loons,
To go and fight mit Sigel.

# We Are Coming, Father Abra'am

Words: James Sloan Gibbon
Music: Patrick Sarsfield Gilmore
Version of "Wearing of The Green"

The heavy losses during the Peninsular campaign were the dark days for the Union cause. On July 2, 1862, Lincoln issued a call for three hundred thousand more soldiers. In response to Lincoln's appeal, James Sloan Gibbon wrote this ringing call to arms—"We Are Coming, Father Abra'am." Gibbon was a Quaker "with a reasonable leaning, however, toward wrath in cases of emergency," as his son-in-law, Mr. James H. Morse, neatly put it in a letter to Brander Matthews. * The composer of the music, Patrick Sarsfield Gilmore, was the Band Master of the Union Armies.

1. We are com - ing, Fath - er A - braam, three hun - dred thou - sand more, From — Mis - sis - sip - pi's wind - ing stream and from New Eng - land's shore; We — leave our plows and work - shops, our wives and chil - dren dear, With — hearts too full for ut - ter - ance, with

*Matthews, Brander, *Pen and Ink*

2.

If you look across the hilltops
   That meet the northern sky,
Long moving lines of rising dust
   Your vision may descry;
And now the wind, an instant,
   Tears the cloudy veil aside,
And floats aloft our spangled flag
   In glory and in pride;
And bayonets in the sunlight gleam,
   And bands brave music pour,
We are coming, Father Abra'am,
   Three hundred thousand more.

*Chorus:* We are coming, etc.

3.

If you look all up our valleys,
   Where the growing harvests shine,
You may see our sturdy farmerboys
   Fast forming into line;
And children from their mothers' knees
   Are pulling at the weeds,
And learning how to reap and sow
   Against their country's needs;
And a farewell group stands weeping
   At every cottage door,
We are coming, Father Abra'am
   Three hundred thousand more.

*Chorus:* We are coming, etc.

4.

You have called us, and we're coming,
   By Richmond's bloody tide,
To lay us down for freedom's sake,
   Our brother's bones beside;
Or from foul treason's savage group
   To wrench the murderous blade,
And in the face of foreign foes
   Its fragments to parade;
Six hundred thousand loyal men
   And true have gone before,
We are coming, Father Abra'am,
   Three hundred thousand more.

*Chorus:* We are coming, etc.

# We'll Fight for Uncle Abe

Words: C. E. Pratt
Music: Frederick Buckley

This rollicking and spirited tune was composed in the style of the minstrel stage songs. Frederick Buckley was the leader of that prominent Minstrel Troupe, "The Buckley Serenaders."

The use of such designations as "Father" and "Uncle" reflects the affection of the people for President Lincoln.

Slow and steady

1. Way down in old Var-gin - ni, I sup - pose you all do know, They have

tried to bust the Un - ion But they find it is no go, The

yan - kee boys are start - ing out de Un - ion for to sabe, And we're

go - ing down to Wash - ing - ton, To fight for Un - cle Abe.

**Chorus**

Rip, rap, flip, flap, Strap your knap-sacks on your back For we're a gwine to Wash-ing-ton, To

1. fight for Un - cle Abe.

2. fight for Un - cle Abe.

2.

There is General Grant at Vicksburg,
    Just see what he has done,
He has taken sixty cannon
    And made the Rebels run,
And next he will take Richmond
    I'll bet you half a dollar
And if he catches Gen'ral Johnson
    Oh won't he make him holler.

*Chorus*: Rip, Rap, Flip, Flap, etc.

3.

The season now is coming
   When the roads begin to dry,
Soon the army of the Potomac
   Will make the rebels fly,
For General McClellan,
   He's the man the Union for to sabe,
O! Hail Columbia's right side up,
   And so's your Uncle Abe.

*Chorus*: Rip, Rap, Flip, Flap, etc.

4.

You may talk of Southern chivalry
   And Cotton being king,
But I guess before the war is done
   You'll think another thing.
They say that recognition
   Will the rebel country sabe,
But Johnny Bull and Mister France
   Are 'fraid of Uncle Abe.

*Chorus*: Rip, Rap, Flip, Flap, etc.

# He's Gone to the Arms of Abraham

Words and Music:
Septimus Winner

This draftee was not too anxious to get into the army and his sweetheart is very well aware of his feelings.

1. My true love is a sol-dier In the ar-my now to-day, It

was the cru-el war that made him Have to go a-way; The

"draft" it was that took him, And it was a "heav-y blow," It

took him for a Con - script, But he did - n't want to go.

**Chorus**

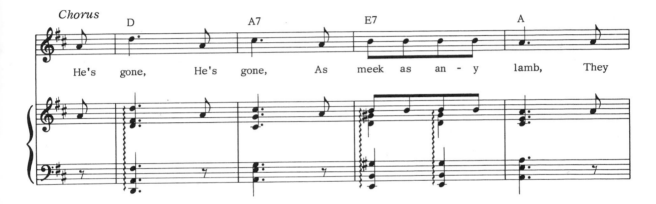

He's gone, He's gone, As meek as an - y lamb, They

took him, yes, they took him, to the arms of A - bra - ham. ham.

2.

He's gone to be a soldier,
    With a knapsack on his back,
A fightin' for the Union
    And a livin' on "hard tack."
Oh, how he look'd like Christian,
    In the Pilgrim's Progress shown,
With a bundle on his shoulders,
    But with nothin' of his own.

*Chorus*: He's gone, etc.

3.

Oh, should he meet a rebel,
    A pointin' with his gun,
I hope he may have courage
    To "take care of number one."
If I were him, I'd offer
    The fellow but a dram;
For what's the use of dying
    Just for Jeff or Abraham?

*Chorus*: He's gone, etc.

4.

Indeed, to be a soldier,
  It is so very hard,
For when a fellow has his fun
  They poke him on the guard:
One day he shot a rooster,
  The captain thought it wrong;
And so to punish him they made
  Him picket all night long.

*Chorus*: He's gone, etc.

5.

I haven't got a lover now,
  I haven't got a beau;
They took him as a raw recruit,
  But mustered him, I know:
He's nothing but a private,
  And not for war inclined,
Although a hard old nut to crack
  A colonel you might find.

*Chorus*: He's gone, etc.

6.

My true love is a soldier,
  Upon the battle-ground,
And if he ever should be lost
  I hope he may be found;
If he should fall a fightin'
  Upon the battle-plain,
I hope some other chap may come
  And pick him up again.

*Chorus*: He's gone, etc.

# To Canaan
## Song of the Six Hundred Thousand

Words and Music:
C. A. Brainard, E. A. Kelly, W. E. Thayer

After Lincoln's call for three hundred thousand additional troops in 1862, the number was soon raised to six hundred thousand. This marching hymn is a response to that call. The lyrics show devotion, faith in the Lord, and the hope that liberty will live forever in a reunited land.

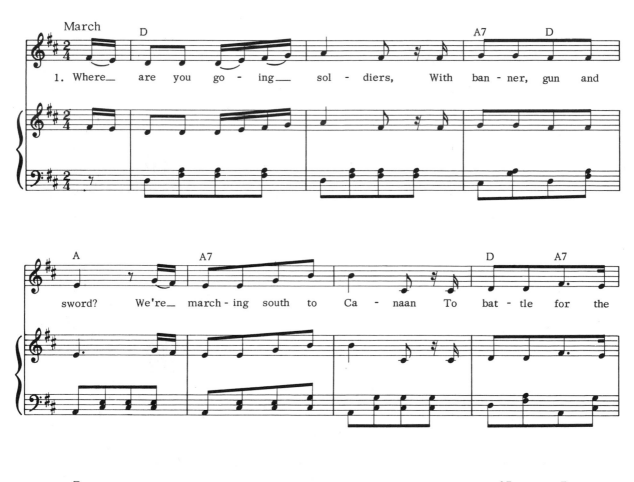

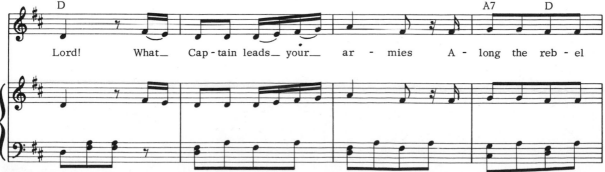

1. Where are you go-ing sol-diers, With ban-ner, gun and sword? We're march-ing south to Ca-naan To bat-tle for the Lord! What Cap-tain leads your ar-mies A-long the reb-el

2.

What flag is this you carry
　　Along the sea and shore?
The same our grandsires lifted up,
　　The same our fathers bore!
In many a battle's tempest
　　It shed the crimson rain, —
What God has woven in his loom,
　　Let no man rend in twain!

*Chorus*:

　　To Canaan, to Canaan
　　The Lord has led us forth,
　　To plant upon the rebel towers
　　The banners of the North!
　　(Repeat these four lines)

### 3.

What troup is this that follows,
    All armed with picks and spades?
These are the swarthy bondsmen,
    The iron-skin brigades!
They'll pile up freedom's breastwork,
    They'll scoop out rebels' graves.
Who then will be their owner,
    And march them off for slaves.

*Chorus*:

    To Canaan, to Canaan
    The Lord has led us forth,
    To strike upon the captive's chain
    The hammers of the North!
    (Repeat these four lines)

### 4.

What song is this you're singing?
    The same that Israel sung
When Moses led the mighty choir,
    And Miriam's timbrel rung
To Canaan!   To Canaan!
    The priests and maidens cried
To Canaan!   To Canaan!
    The people's voice replied.

*Chorus*:

    To Canaan, to Canaan
    The Lord has led us forth,
    To thunder through its adder dens,
    The anthems of the North!
    (Repeat these four lines)

### 5.

When Canaan's hosts are scattered,
    And all her walls lie flat.
What follows next in order?
    The Lord will see to that!
We'll break the tyrant's scepter,
    We'll build the people's throne,
When half the world is Freedom's
    Then all the world's our own!

*Chorus*:

    To Canaan, to Canaan
    The Lord has led us forth,
    To sweep the rebel threshing floors
    A whirlwind from the North!
    (Repeat these four lines)

# Grafted into the Army

Words and Music:
Henry Clay Work

With conscription came a storm of protest on both sides. "Unconstitutional," shouted the politicians from North and South. Riots in New York City lasted for four days.

From Henry Clay Work's pen came many favorite songs, such as: "Marching Through Georgia", "Wake Nicodemus" and "Kingdom Coming," all of which are in this collection. This song brings forth the humor and pathos of a mother pleading for her son who was "grafted" into the army anyway.

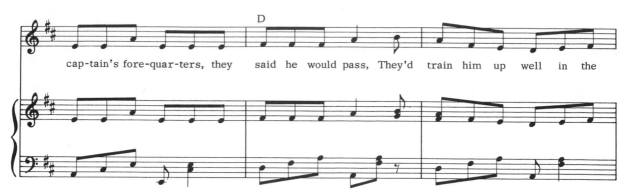

cap-tain's fore-quar-ters, they said he would pass, They'd train him up well in the

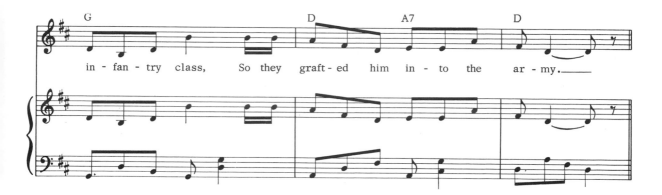

in - fan - try class, So they graft - ed him in - to the ar - my.___

*Chorus*

Oh Jim -my, fare-well! Your broth - ers fell Way down in Al - a - bar- my;___ I

thought they would spare__ a lone wid-der's heir, But they graft-ed him in-to the ar-my.___

2.

Drest up in his uni-corn — dear little chap;
They have grafted him into the army;
It seems but a day since he sot in my lap,
But they grafted him into the army.
And these are the trousies he used to wear —
Them very same buttons — the patch and the tear —
But what if the ducky should up and die
Now they've grafted him into the army.

*Chorus*:  Oh Jimmy, farewell! etc.

3.

Now in my provisions I see him revealed —
They have grafted him into the army;
A picket beside the contented field,
They have grafted him into the army.
He looks kinder sickish — begins to cry —
A big volunteer standing right in his eye!
Oh what if the ducky should up and die
Now they've grafted him into the army.

*Chorus*:  Oh Jimmy, farewell! etc.

# Come in out of the Draft
## or
## How Are You Conscript?

Words: Ednor Rossiter
Music: B. Frank Walthers

When the bounty system failed to furnish the necessary numbers, both sections resorted to the last expedient—conscription. The Confederacy was first and Jefferson Davis signed a conscription act on April 16, 1862. After much debate, Congress passed a conscription act on March 3, 1863. In the South, exemption from the service could be gained by supplying an acceptable substitute or by paying the government a fee not to exceed $300.00. Those who were between the ages of twenty and forty-five and unmarried, or twenty and thirty-five and married were subject to military duty.

This is a comical song describing the problems of one bachelor who is over thirty-five, and is "Respectfully Dedicated to all Disconsolate Conscripts." It was published in 1863.

1. As it was rath-er warm, I thought the oth-er day, I'd find some cool-er place The sum-mer months to stay; I had not long been gone When a pa-per to me came, And in the list of con-scripts I

chanced to see my name, I showed it to my friends, And at me they all laughed, They said "How are you con-script? Come in out of the draft." draft."

### 2.
Oh, soon I hurried home, for I felt rather blue;
I thought I'd ask my dad what I had better do;
Says he, "You are not young, — you're over thirty-five:
The best thing you can do, sir, is — go and take a bride."
    My mother on me smiled, my brother at me laugh'd,
    And said, "How are you, conscript? — come in out of the draft."

### 3.
I soon made up my mind that I would take a wife;
For she could save my cash, and I could save my life.
I call'd upon a friend, I offer'd her my hand,
But she said she couldn't see it, for she loved some other man.
    She told it to her man, and at me they both laugh'd,
    And said, "How are you, conscript? — come in out of the draft."

### 4.
So next I advertised, and soon a chap I found
Who said that he would go for just two hundred down.
I took him home to sleep. Says I, "Now I'm all right."
But, when I woke, I found that he'd robb'd me in the night!
    I went and told the mayor: the people round me laugh'd,
    And said, "How are you, conscript? — come in out of the draft."

### 5.

I to the provost's went, my "notice" in my hand;
I found a crowd around, and with it took my stand.
I waited there till night, from early in the morn,
And, when I got inside, my pocket-book was gone!
   I thought I should go mad! but everybody laugh'd,
    And said, "How are you, conscript? — come in out of the draft."


### 6.

I've tried to get a wife, I've tried to get a "sub,"
But what I next shall do, now, really, is the "rub."
My money's almost gone, and I am nearly daft:
Will some one tell me what to do to get out of the draft?
   I've ask'd my friends all round, but at me they all laugh'd,
    And said, "How are you, conscript? — come in out of the draft."

# How Are You, Conscript?

Words and Music:
Frank Wilder

This humorous song is about a would-be draft dodger. He doesn't have the necessary "three hundred greenbacks to pony up and pay" which would keep him out for a while, so the Provost Marshall has him in a very tight place.

1. "How are you, Con- script?" "How are you to - day?" The
Pro- vost Mar- shal's got you in a ver - y "tight place" they say! But
O, you should not mind it Nor breathe an - oth - er sigh, For you're

only going to Dixie To fight and "mind your eye" O____

*Chorus*

How are you, Con-script? How are you to-day? The Pro-vost Mar-shal's got you in a

ver-y "tight place," they say! ver-y "tight place," they say!

**2.**

"How are you, Conscript?"
  "How are you, my boy?"
I 'spose you take it rather hard,
  Since you're your mother's joy.
But "Uncle Sam" says you're the one
  To "go in" hip and thigh,
For you're only going to Dixie
  To fight and "mind your eye" O

*Chorus*: How are you, Conscript? etc.

**3.**

"How are you, Conscript?"
  "How are you, I say?"
Have you got "three hundred greenbacks"
  To "pony up" and pay?
If not you are "a goner"
  Now don't you fret and cry,
For you're only going to Dixie
  To fight and "mind your eye" O

*Chorus*: How are you, Conscript? etc.

4.

"How are you, Conscript?"
   "How are you today?"
You'll give us all a "lock of hair"
   Before you go away.
And when you do come home again,
   You'll "see it" same as I,
For you're only going to Dixie
   To fight and "mind your eye" O

*Chorus*:  How are you, Conscript? etc.

# The Invalid Corps

Words and Music:
Frank Wilder

If you couldn't get a substitute or pay the fee, your only chance of staying out of the army was to fail the medical. This humorous song is about a conscript who hopes to be rejected. He is examined by the medical officer, gets his "4F" and sings about his experience.

Lively

I___ want-ed much to go to war, And went to be ex - am-ined; The___
sur-geon looked me o'er and o'er, My back and chest he ham-mered. Said
he, "You're not the man for me, Your lungs are much af-fect-ed, And

like - wise both your eyes are cock'd And oth - er - wise de - fect - ed."

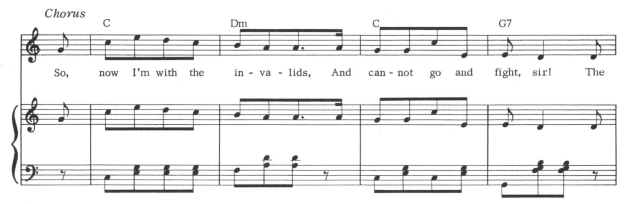

*Chorus*

So, now I'm with the in - va - lids, And can - not go and fight, sir! The

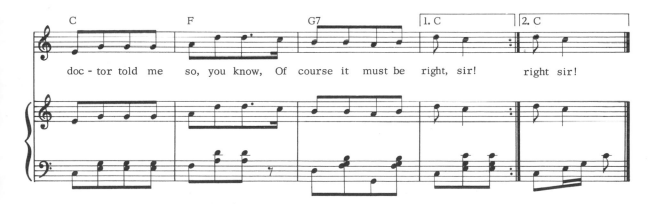

doc - tor told me so, you know, Of course it must be right, sir! right sir!

2.

While I was there a host of chaps
    For reasons were exempted,
Old "pursy," he was laid aside,
    To pass he had attempted.
The Doctor said, "I do not like
    Your corporosity, sir!
You'll 'breed a famine' in the camp
    Wherever you might be, sir!"

*Chorus*: So, now I'm with, etc.

3.

There came a fellow, mighty tall,
  A "knock-kneed overgrowner,"
The Doctor said, "I aint got time
  To take and look you over."
Next came along a little chap,
  Who was 'bout two foot nothing;
The Doctor said, "You'd better go
  And tell your marm you're coming."

*Chorus:* So, now I'm with, etc.

4.

Some had the ticerdolerreou,
  Some what they call "brown critters,"
And some were "lank and lazy" too;
  Some were too "fond of bitters."
Some had "cork legs" and some "one eye,"
  With backs deformed and crooked;
I'll bet you'd laugh'd till you had cried,
  To see how "cute" they looked.

*Chorus:* So, now I'm with, etc.

# Army Life In Camp

# Hard Crackers Come Again No More

Words: Anonymous
Music: Stephen Collins Foster
      "Hard Times Come Again No More"

    Despite all the gripes about rations and hardships on the march, the boys in Blue and Grey joked about their tribulations in an earthy humor.  This song has been called the "musical bellyache" from the Army of the Potomac.

Let us close our game of pok-er, Take our tin cups in hand, While we gath-er round the cook's tent door Where dry mum-mies of hard crack-ers Are giv-en to each man; Oh, hard crack-ers come a-gain no more!

**2.**

There's a hungry, thirsty soldier,
Who wears his life away,
With torn clothes, whose better days are o'er;
He is sighing now for whiskey,
And, with throat as dry as hay,
Sings, "Hard crackers come again no more."

*Chorus*: 'Tis the song and the sigh, etc.

**3.**

'Tis the song that is uttered
In camp by night and day,
'Tis the wail that is mingled with each snore;
'Tis the sighing of the soul
For spring chickens far away,
"Oh, hard crackers come again no more."

*Chorus*: 'Tis the song and the sigh, etc.

# Boys, Keep Your Powder Dry
## Dedicated
## "To the Southern Boys"

Words and Music:
Fr. C. Mayer

Stormy weather and mud often imperiled the quantity and quality of ammunition. Keeping the supply dry could mean the difference between life and death—and success or failure of a major campaign. Since purchases from Europe became more difficult because of the blockade, the infantrymen were cautioned to keep the "stuff" dry.

Spirited

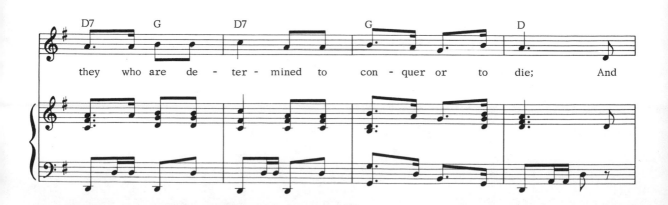

Can'st tell who lost the bat - tle, off in the coun - cil's field? Not they who strug - gle brave - ly, Not they who nev - er yield, Not they who are de - ter - mined to con - quer or to die; And

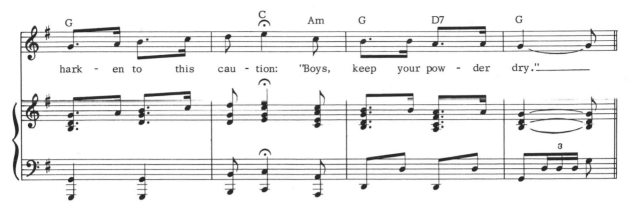

hark - en to this cau - tion: "Boys, keep your pow - der dry."_____

*Chorus*

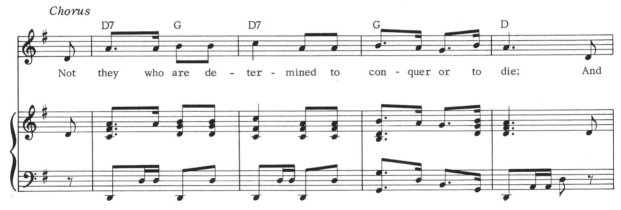

Not they who are de - ter - mined to con - quer or to die; And

hark - en to this cau - tion: "Boys, keep your pow - der dry."_____ dry."_____

2.
The foe awaits you yonder,
    He may await you here;
Have brave hearts, stand with courage,
    Be strangers, all, to fear;
And when the charge is given,
    Be ready at the cry.
Look well each to his priming —
    "Boys, keep your powder dry."

*Chorus*: Not they who are, etc.

3.

Does a lov'd one home await you,
    Who wept to see you go,
Whom with a kiss imprinted
    You left with sacred vow
You'd come again, when warfare
    And arms are all laid by,
To take her to your bosom?
    "Boys, keep your powder dry."

*Chorus*:  Not they who are, etc.

4.

Does a father home await you?
    A sister whom you love?
A mother who hast reared you,
    And prayed to Him above:
"Protect my boy, preserve him,
    And when the battle's done,
Send to his weeping mother,
    Bereft, her darling son!"

*Chorus*:  Not they who are, etc.

5.

The name of Freedom calls you,
    The names of martyr'd sires,
And Liberty's imploring
    From all her hallowed fires.
Can you withstand their calling?
    You can not pass them by —
You can not?  Now, charge fiercely!
    "Boys, keep your powder dry."

*Chorus*:  Not they who are, etc.

Tenting To-Night

On The Old Camp Ground.

Words & Music by Walter Kittredge.

40

BOSTON:
Published by OLIVER DITSON COMPANY. 449 & 451 Washington St.

NEW-YORK: C.H.DITSON & CO. 867 BROADWAY

CHICAGO.ILL LYON & HEALY, COR STATE & MONROE STS.

PHILADELPHIA: J.E.DITSON & CO. 1228 CHESTNUT ST

BOSTON: JOHN C HAYNES & CO 33 COURT & 694 WASHINGTON STS

Copyright 1890 by Oliver Ditson Company. Boston

# Tenting on the Old Camp Ground

Words and Music:
Walter Kittredge

This was one of the most popular songs on both sides. It is reported that its appeal was so strong that officers had to restrain their men from singing it at night because they would divulge their positions on the field.

Walter Kittredge was a concert ballad singer from New Hampshire. Although he was deferred from army service, this did not prevent him from singing this song to the Union Army at Camps in the field.

2.

We've been tenting tonight on the old Camp ground,
  Thinking of days gone by,
Of the lov'd ones at home that gave us the hand,
  And the tear that said "Good bye!"

*Chorus*:  Many are the hearts, etc.

3.

We are tired of war on the old Camp ground,
  Many are dead and gone,
Of the brave and true who've left their homes,
  Others been wounded long,

*Chorus*:  Many are the hearts, etc.

4.

We've been fighting today on the old Camp ground,
  Many are lying near;
Some are dead, and some are dying,
  Many are in tears.

*Chorus*: *(After Last Verse)*
  Many are the hearts that are weary tonight,
  Wishing for the war to cease,
  Many are the hearts looking for the right
  To see the dawn of peace.
  Dying tonight, Dying tonight,
  Dying on the old Camp ground.

# The Upidee Song

Words: D. G. Knight
Music: A. E. Blackmar

This jolly Confederate song establishes the bugler as the "killjoy" of the army. The familiar tones regulate the soldier's life, disturb him at meals, and interrupt the few moments of leisure that occasionally come along. The poem apes Longfellow's "Excelsior."

Quite fast

1. The shades of night were fall - ing fast, Tra la la! tra la la! The bu - gler blew his well - known blast, Tra la la la la. No mat - ter, be there rain or snow, That bu - gler still is bound to blow,

*Chorus*

U - pi de - i de - i da! U - pi de! U - pi da!

U - pi de - i de - i da! U - pi de - i da. da.____

### 2.
He saw, as in their bunks they lay,
   Tra, la, la! tra, la, la!
How soldiers spent the dawning day.
   Tra, la, la, la, la.
"There's too much comfort there,"said he,
"And so I'll blow the 'Reveille'."

*Chorus*: Upi dei, etc.

### 3.
In nice log huts he saw the light,
   Tra, la, la! tra, la, la!
Of cabin fires, warm and bright,
   Tra, la, la, la, la.
The sight afforded him no heat,
And so he sounded the "Retreat."

*Chorus*: Upi dei, etc.

### 4.
Upon the fire he spied a pot,
   Tra, la, la! tra, la, la!
Choicest viands smoking hot,
   Tra, la, la, la, la.
Says he, "You shan't enjoy the stew,"
So "Boots and Saddles" loudly blew.

*Chorus*: Upi dei, etc.

### 5.
They scarce their half-cooked meal begin
   Tra, la, la! tra, la, la!
Ere orderly cries out, "Fall in!"
   Tra, la, la, la, la.
Then off they march through mud and rain,
P'raps only to march back again.

*Chorus*: Upi dei, etc.

### 6.
But soldiers, you are made to fight,
   Tra, la, la! tra, la, la!
To starve all day and march all night,
   Tra, la, la, la, la.
Perchance if you get bread and meat
That bugler will not let you eat.

*Chorus*: Upi dei, etc.

### 7.
Oh, hasten then, that glorious day
   Tra, la, la! tra, la, la!
When buglers shall no longer play;
   Tra, la, la, la, la.
When we, through Peace, shall be set free
From "Tattoo," "Taps" and "Reveille."

*Chorus*: Upi dei, etc.

# Think of Your Head in the Morning
## Dedicated
## "To all commissaries, quartermasters, surgeons in the Confederate Army"

Words and Music:
Charles L. Ward

Excessive drinking was not uncommon with the soldiers on both sides. An order from the War Department in 1862 stated, "it is the cause of nearly every evil from which we suffer . . . our guard houses are filled by it." Commanders were urged to suppress drunkenness with harsh punishment. Naturally, the bootleg stuff was pretty vile and the Rebs described it as "pop-skull," "old red eye," and "bust head." The Yank's liquor wasn't any better. He referred to it as "bark juice," "tar water," and lamp oil."*

1. Tom Jen - nings who nev - er could drink - ing a - void Tho'
vows he was al - ways - a - mak - ing; But af - ter each bout he was
ev - er an - noyed with a ner - vous - ness and a head ach - ing. Go - ing

*Wiley, B. I., *The Life of Johnny Reb*, p. 40-41
Bobbs Merrill Co., by permission

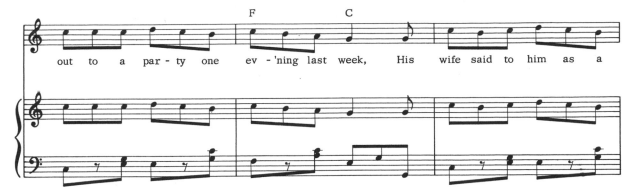

out to a par - ty one ev - 'ning last week, His wife said to him as a

warn - ing, "Be care - ful, dear Thom - as, and mind what you take, And

*Chorus*

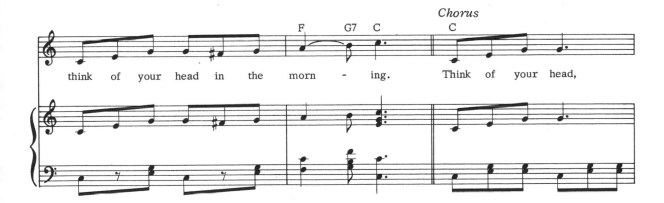

think of your head in the morn - ing. Think of your head,

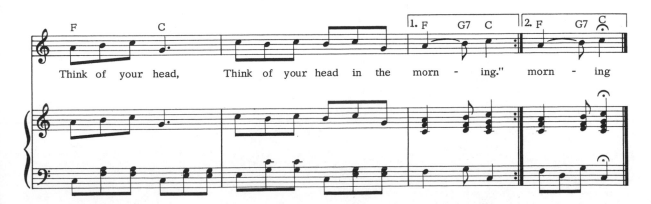

Think of your head, Think of your head in the morn - ing." morn - ing

### 2.

He promised sincerely to bear it in mind,
And at dinner, at first, he was cautious;
And tho very nice he the Sherry did find,
He sipped it as though it were nauseous.
But wine will the best resolutions destroy.
By degrees he forgot his wife's warning,
And he said with each glass, "Tom, (hic) be care(hic)ful my boy,
And think of your head in the morning."

*Chorus*: Think of your head, etc.

### 3.

In the course of the night he was asked for a toast,
And he gave, like a man of discerning,
"Here's the friend we can (hic) trust, and the girl (hic) we love most,
Who will (hic) think of your head in the morning." —
"Bravo," said they, "tis a capital say,"
Then up with their glasses all turning,
"Mr. Jennings' (hic) sentiment, hip, hip, horray." —
Oh, their poor heads in the morning.

*Chorus*: Oh! their poor heads, etc.

### 4.

On leaving the party, with drink nearly blind,
He came 'gainst a pump near a turning,
He turned 'round and said, "Sir, its (hic) very un(hic)kind,
Just think of (hic) my head in (hic) the morning."
Then rolled in the gutter. "It's very illbred;
You might, (hic) Sir, have (hic) given me warning."
All covered with mud, as he lay there he said,
"Shant I look (hic) spruce (hic) in the morning."

*Chorus*: Shant I look spruce, etc.

### 5.

At last he reached home with his hat without brim,
And he spoke to his wife rather fawning,
"I've been (hic) struck by a brute (hic) because I said to him:
To think of my head (hic) in the morning.
Too tipsey for bed as he lay on the floor,
How he caught it for scorning her warning.
"Now aint you ashamed, Sir." "My dear (hic) say no (hic) more,
But think of my head in the morning."

*Chorus*: But think of my head, etc.

# Here's Your Mule

Words and Music:
C. D. Benson

A.W.O.L. was a common problem for the Union and Confederate armies. Whatever reasons there may be, the percentage was substantial on both sides. This very popular, humorous Confederate song blames the "farmer."

Lusty

A Farm - er came to camp___ one day, With milk___ and eggs___ to sell, Up - on___ a mule who oft___ would stray, To where___ no one___ could tell, The Farm - er tir - ed of his tramp, For hours was made the

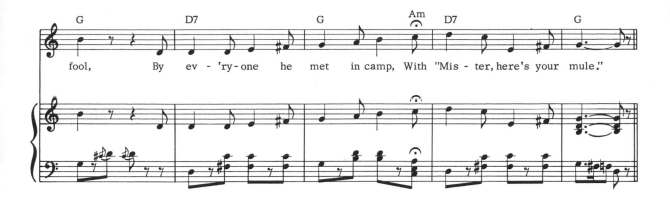

fool, By ev-'ry-one he met in camp, With "Mis-ter, here's your mule."

*Chorus*

Come on,___ come on, Come on,___ old man, And don't___ be made___ a

fool,_____ By ev-'ry-one, You meet___ in camp, With

1. "Mis-ter, here's your mule."___ 2. "Mis-ter, here's your mule."___

**2.**

His eggs and chickens all were gone,
　　Before the break of day,
The "Mule" was heard of all along.
　　That's what the Soldier's say.
And still he hunted all day long,
　　Alas! the witless fool,
Whil'st ev'ry man would sing the song,
　　Of "Mister, here's your Mule."

*Chorus*: Come on, come on, etc.

**3.**

The Soldiers ran in laughing mood,
　　On mischief were intent;
They lifted "Muley" on their back,
　　Around from tent to tent.
Thro' this hole, and that, they push'd
　　His head, — And made a rule,
To shout with humorous voices all,
　　I say! "Mister, here's your Mule."

*Chorus*: Come on, come on, etc.

**4.**

Alas! one day the mule was miss'd,
　　Ah! who could tell his fate?
The Farmer like a man bereft,
　　Search'd early and search'd late.
And as he pass'd from camp to camp
　　With stricken face — the fool
Cried out to ev'ry one he met,
　　Oh! "Mister, where's my Mule."

*Chorus*: Come on, come on, etc.

# Short Rations
## to the
## Corn-Fed Army of Tennessee

Words: Ye Tragic
Music: Ye Comic

The name of "Ye Comic" is still a riddle. But "Ye Tragic" was John Alcee Augustin, a soldier in the Confederate army of Tennessee. He wrote a number of poems during the war and "Short Rations" was timely and popular.

Getting food supplies to the Confederate Army often brought about friction and criticism. Bell Irwin Wiley claims soldiers "often went into combat hungry."* In this song the "Big-Brass" are blamed. Here you can also get some ideas between the lines.

Loud, raucous and energetic

Fair la - dies and maids___ of all a - ges, Lit - tle
girls___ and ca - dets___ how - e'er youth - ful, Home
guards,_ quar-ter-mas - ters and sa - ges, Who___ write for the news-pa-pers so

*Wiley, B. I., *The Life of Johnny Reb*, p. 89
Bobbs Merrill Co., by permission

truth - ful! Clerks, sur - geons and supes,__ leg - is - la - tors, Staff

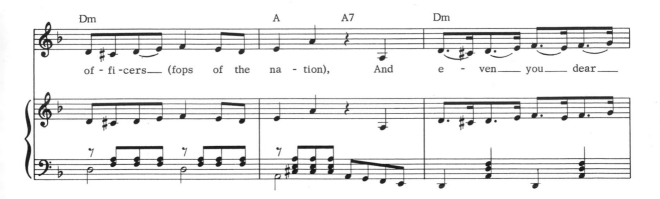

of - fi -cers__ (fops of the na - tion), And e - ven__ you__ dear__

spec - u - la - tors, Come__ list to my song of star - va - tion!

*Chorus*

For we sol - diers have seen some-thing rough - er, Than a

storm,__ a re-treat,__ or a fight, And the bod - y may toil_____ on and suf - fer, With a smile, so the heart is all right!

### 2.

Our bugles had roused up the camp,
    The heavens look'd dismal and dirty,
And the earth look'd unpleasant and damp,
    As a beau on the wrong side of thirty.
We were taking these troubles with quiet,
    When we heard from the mouths of some rash ones,
That the army was all put on diet,
    And the Board had diminished our rations.

*Chorus*: For we soldiers, etc.

### 3.

Reduce our rations at all?
    It was difficult, yet it was done,
We had one meal a day, it was small,
    Are we now, oh! ye gods! to have none?
Oh! ye gentlemen issuing rations,
    Give at least half her own to the State,
Put a curb on your maddening passions,
    And commissaries commisserate!

*Chorus*: For we soldiers, etc.

### 4.

Erewhiles we had chickens and roasters,
    For the fowls and pigs were ferocious,
We would sent them to short Pater Nosters,
    And the deed was not stamped as atrocious;
But since men have been shot for the same,
    We parch corn, it is healthier, but tougher —
The chickens and pigs have got tame,
    But the horses and mules have to suffer.

*Chorus*: For we soldiers, etc.

### 5.

But the "Corn-fed" is proof to all evils,
    Has a joke for all hardships and troubles,
In honor and glory he revels,
    Other fancies he looks on as bubbles!
He is bound to be free, and he knows it,
    Then what cares he for toil and privation!
He is brave, and in battle he shows it,
    And will conquer in spite of starvation.

*Chorus*: For we soldiers, etc.

# Goober Peas

Words: P. Pindar, Esq.
Music: P. Nutt, Esq.

"Soldiering can be a very dull job," says Bell Irwin Wiley in his *Life of Johnny Reb*. From the diary of a Confederate soldier, James Kuykendall, we get this impression:

"None can imagine, who has never experienced a soldier's life, the languor of mind—tediousness of time, as we resume day after day the monotonous duties devolved upon us."*

One way of passing the time, when not on the march or at drill, was to get together around the campfire and enjoy some informal singing. This delightful Confederate song has a spontaneity and simplicity with that spirit of songmaking and rhyme that lets the mind forget the orders, the dust and the blistering feet.

*Wiley, B. I., *The Life of Johnny Reb*, p. 151
Bobbs Merrill Co., by permission

**2.**

When a horseman passes,
   The soldiers have a rule,
To cry out at their loudest,
   "Mister, here's your mule,"
But another pleasure
   Enchantinger than these,
Is wearing out your Grinders,
   Eating goober peas!

*Chorus*: Peas! Peas! etc.

**3.**

Just before the battle,
   The Gen'ral hears a row,
He says, "The Yanks are coming,
   I hear their rifles now."
He turns around in wonder,
   And what do you think he sees?
The Georgia Militia,
   Eating goober peas!

*Chorus*: Peas! Peas! etc.

**4.**

I think my song has lasted
   Almost long enough,
The subject's interesting,
   But rhymes are mighty rough,
I wish the war was over
   When free from rags and fleas,
We'd kiss our wives and sweethearts
   And gobble goober peas!

*Chorus*: Peas! Peas! etc.

# The Army Bean

**Words:** Anonymous
**Music:** Tune of "Sweet Bye and Bye"

To the scientist the bean is a "leguminous" plant which is cultivated for food. But to the soldiers on both sides it was a staple ration that brought about many rhymes and gripes. At times the soldiers would pool their beans and bake them in a "bean hole" in the ground. The flavor was a welcome relief from "hard-tack" and mash.

Moderato

1. There's a spot that the sol - diers all love, The____ mess tent's the place that we mean, And the dish we best like to see there Is the old - fash - ioned white ar - my bean.

*Chorus*

'Tis the bean that we mean, And we'll eat as we ne'er ate be-

fore; The ar - my bean, nice and clean, We'll

stick to our beans ev - er - more. more.

2.

Now the bean in its primitive state
Is a plant we have all often met;
And when cooked in the old army style
It has charms we can never forget.

*Chorus*: 'Tis the bean, etc.

3.

The German is fond of sauerkraut,
The potato is loved by the Mick,
But the soldiers have long since found out
That through life to our beans we should stick.

*Chorus*: 'Tis the bean, etc.

# Army Bugs

To the same tune, "Sweet Bye and Bye," the soldiers sang about the fight against the lice. These "Cooties" and what the Confederates called "tigers" and "Bragg's bodyguard," were numerous on both sides. Killing them was called "fighting under the black flag."

Soldiers sing of their beans and canteens,
Of the coffee in old army cup,
Why not mention the small friends we've seen
Always trying to chew armies up?

*Chorus:*
　　Those firm friends, tireless friends,
　　Hardly ever neglecting their hugs,
　　Their regard never ends,
　　How they loved us, those old army bugs!

# Tramp! Tramp! Tramp!

## The Prisoners' Hope

Words and Music:
George F. Root

This is another one of Root's most popular songs. For the many thousands of Union soldiers in Confederate prisons, and for the folks back home, it stirred the spirit of hope as the Union armies advanced. We still sing it today, perhaps because of its lively rhythms.

In a strong, steady manner

1. In the pris - on cell I sit, Think - ing Moth - er dear, of you, And our

bright and hap -py house so far a - way, And the tears they fill my eyes Spite of

all that I can do, Tho' I try to cheer my com-rades and be gay.

*Chorus*

Tramp, tramp, tramp, the boys are march — ing, Cheer up com - rades, they will come; And be - neath the star - ry flag We shall breathe the air a - gain, Of the free - land in our own be - lov - ed home. 2. In the home.

2.

In the battle front we stood
When their fiercest charge they made,
And they swept us off a hundred men or more;
But before we reach'd their lines
They were beaten back dismayed,
And we heard the cry of vict'ry o'er and o'er.

*Chorus:* Tramp, tramp, tramp, etc.

3.

So within the prison cell,
We are waiting for the day
That shall come to open wide the iron door;
And the hollow eye grows bright,
And the poor heart almost gay,
As we think of seeing home and friends once more.

*Chorus:* Tramp, tramp, tramp, etc.

# Part Three

# *Battles and Soldiers*

# God Bless the Old Sixth Corps

Words and Music:
Thomas P. Ryder

The Sixth Corps was formed on October 18, 1862 during the Peninsular campaign. It was part of the Army of the Potomac. This Corps distinguished itself in the Maryland campaign, at Culpeper, and in battles together with Sheridan's cavalry. The song recalls the death of its "noble" leader, General Sedgwick, and the brave who "fought and fell." Other commanders of the Corps were Generals Franklin, Smith and Slocum.

1. God bless____ our no - ble ar - my! The hearts____ are strong____ and

brave____ That have will - ing come___ our stand - ard From trea - son's grasp to

save;____ But from the West - ern Prai - rie To At - lan - tic's rock - y

shore,_____ The tru - est, no - blest hearts of all Are_ in the Old_ Sixth Corps._

*Chorus*

Then, ere_ we part_ to - night, boys, We'll sing_ one song_ the

more,_____ With cho - rus swell - ing loud and clear, God_

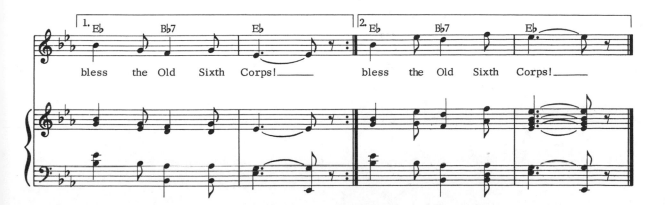

1. bless the Old Sixth Corps!_____ 2. bless the Old Sixth Corps!_____

2.

In the thickest of the battle,
  Where the cannon's fiery breath
Smites many a strong heart pressing
  On to victory or death!
The foremost in the conflict,
  The last to say  "tis o'er"
Who know not what it is to yield
  You'll find the "Old Sixth Corps."

*Chorus*:  Then, ere we part, etc.

3.

There's many a brave man lying
  Where he nobly fought and fell;
There's many a mother sighing
  For the sons she loved so well;
And the Southern winds are breathing
  A requiem where they lie;
O, the gallant followers of the cross
  Are not afraid to die!

*Chorus*:  Then, ere we part, etc.

4.

Our truest, bravest heart is gone,
  And we remember well
The bitter anguish of that day
  When noble Sedgwick fell;
But there is still another left
  To lead us to the fight,
And with a hearty three times three
  We'll cheer our gallant Wright.

*Chorus*:  Then, ere we part, etc.

5.

Then on! still onward will we press,
  Till treason's voice we still,
And proudly waves the "Stripes and Stars"
  On ev'ry Southern hill.
We'll struggle till our flag is safe
  And honored as before;
And men in future times shall say,
  "God bless the Old Sixth Corps."

*Chorus*:  Then, ere we part, etc.

# Ellsworth Avengers

Words: Anonymous
Music: "Annie Lisle"

Colonel Elmer E. Ellsworth commanded the 11th Regiment of the New York Fire Zouaves and was one of the first casualties of the war. He was fatally shot in May, 1861, while tearing down a secessionist flag in Alexandria as Federal troops were entering Virginia, securing Arlington Heights. The Colonel was a personal friend of President Lincoln.

The song describes the incident and pays tribute to Ellsworth and the cause for which he fought. The tune is credited to H. R. Thompson, a very successful song writer of the period.

1. Down where the pa - triot ar - my, Near Po - to - mac's side,
Guards the glo - rious cause of free - dom, gal - lant Ells - worth died;
Brave was the no - ble Chief - tain, At his coun - try's call,

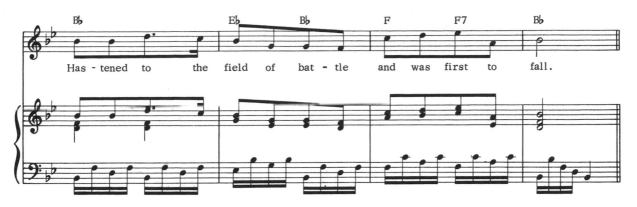

Has - tened to the field of bat - tle and was first to fall.

*Chorus*

Strike, free-men, for the Un - ion, Sheath your swords no more;

While re-mains in arms a trai - tor, On Co - lum-bia's shore. shore.

2.

Entering the traitor city
  With his soldiers true,
Leading up the Zouave columns;
  Fixed became his view.
See that rebel flag is floating
  O'er yon building tall!
Spoke he, while his dark eye glistened,
  "Boys, that flag must fall!"

*Chorus:* Strike, freemen, etc.

**3.**

Quickly from its proud position
   That base flag was torn,
Trampled 'neath the feet of freemen,
   Circling Ellsworth's form;
See him bear it down the landing,
   Past the traitors door,
Hear him groan;  Oh! God, they've shot him,
   Ellsworth is no more.

*Chorus*:  Strike, freemen, etc.

**4.**

First to fall, thou youthful martyr,
   Hapless was thy fate;
Hastened we as thy avengers
   From thy native State.
Speed we on from town and city,
   Not for wealth or fame;
But because we love the Union,
   And our Ellsworth name.

*Chorus*:  Strike, freemen, etc.

**5.**

Traitors hands shall never sunder
   That for which you died;
Hear the oath our lips now utter,
   Those our nation's pride.
By our hopes of yon bright heaven,
   By the land we love,
By the God who reigns above us,
   We'll avenge thy blood.

*Chorus*:  Strike, freemen, etc.

# The *Cumberland's* Crew

Words and Music:
Anonymous

In 1862, the Navy was enforcing the blockade of Southern ports which was declared by Lincoln, and the *Cumberland*, under the command of Lt. George Morris, was patrolling the waters off Newport News, Va. She was rammed and sunk by the Southern ironclad ship, *Merrimac*. It was reported that 117 survived from a crew of 346. This song is a tribute to the heroes who gave their lives for the cause, for as their ship was sinking they sang:

"God bless our dear banner—the red, white and blue;
We'll die by our guns," cried the *Cumberland* crew.

Slow, narrative style

1. O ship-mates come__ gath - er and join in my dit - ty, Of a ter - ri-ble bat - tle that hap - pen'd of late; Let each Un - ion__ Tar shed a tear of his pit - y When he thinks of the once gal - lant

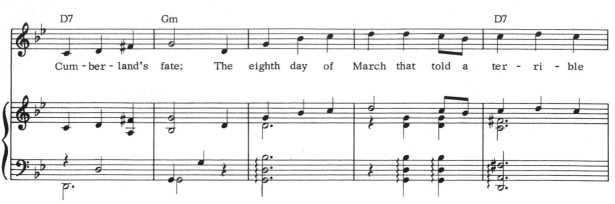

Cum - ber - land's fate; The eighth day of March that told a ter - ri - ble

sto - ry, When man - y a brave Tar to this world bid a - dieu; Our

flag_____ was___ wrapt in a man - tle of___ glo - ry, By the

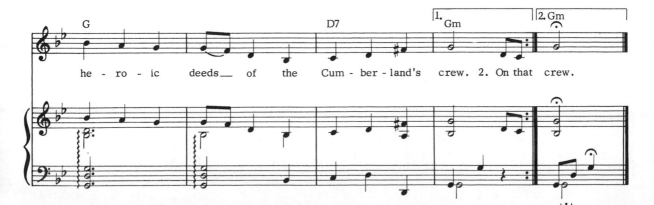

he - ro - ic deeds___ of the Cum - ber - land's crew. 2. On that crew.

2.

On that ill-fated day about ten in the morning,
   The day it was clear, and bright shone the sun;
The drums of the Cumberland sounded a warning,
   That told ev'ry seaman to stand by his gun;
For an ironclad Frigate, down on us came bearing,
   And high in the air, the rebel flag flew,
Her pennant of treason; she proudly was nearing,
   Determined to conquer the Cumberland's crew.
(Repeat last two lines)

3.

Now, up spoke the Captain—with stern resolution,
   Saying, "Boys, of this Monster now don't be dismayed!
We'll swear to maintain our beloved Constitution,
   And to die for our country—we are not afraid!
We'll fight for the Union, our cause it is glorious;
   By the Stars and the Stripes we'll stand ever true;
We'll sink at our quarters, or conquer victorious!"
   He was answered by cheers from the Cumberland's crew.
(Repeat last two lines)

4.

Our noble ship fired huge guns dreadful thunder,
   Her broadsides like hail on the rebel did pour;
The people did gaze on—struck with terror and wonder,
   And the shot struck her sides and glanced harmlessly o'er.
But the pride of our Navy could never be daunted,
   Though our decks with the dead and the wounded did strew;
And the Star Spangled Banner, how proudly it flaunted;
   It was nailed to the mast by the Cumberland's crew.
(Repeat last two lines)

5.

They fought us three hours with stern resolution,
   Till these rebels found cannon could never decide;
For the flag of Secession had no power to quell them
   Though the blood from our scuppers did crimson the tide
She struck us amid-ships, our planks they did sever,
   Her sharp iron-prow pierced our noble ship through;
And they cried, as they sunk in that dark rolling river,
   "We'll die at our guns!" cried the Cumberland's crew.
(Repeat last two lines)

6.

Slowly she sank in the dark rolling waters.
   Their voices on earth will ne'er be heard any more;
They'll be wept by Columbia's brave sons and fair daughters,
   May their blood be avenged on Virginia's old shore;
And if ever our Sailors in battle assemble,
   God bless our dear banner—"The Red, White and Blue!"
Beneath its proud folds we'll cause tyrants to tremble,
   Or "Sink at our guns" like the Cumberland's crew.
(Repeat last two lines)

# The *Alabama*

Words: E. King
Music: F. W. Rosier

According to Henry S. Commager, "the *Alabama* was the most notorious cruiser that James Bulloch had had built at Liverpool for the Confederacy." She was completely outfitted in the middle of 1862 and captained by Raphael Semmes. In a period of two years this "terror of the sea" captured or destroyed over 80 merchantmen and one warship. * This jovial song is about the exploits of the *Alabama*.

With majesty

1. The wind blows off yon rock-y__ shore, Boys, set your sails all free; And soon our boom-ing can-non's roar Shall ring out mer-ri-ly. Run up your bunt-ing taut-a-peak, And swear, lads, to de-fend her; 'Gainst

*Commager, Henry S., *The Blue and The Gray*, pp. 873-74
Bobbs Merrill Co.

ev - 'ry foe, Where - 'er we go, Our mot - to "No Sur - ren - der."

*Chorus*

Then sling the bowl, drink ev, - 'ry soul, A toast to the Al - a - ba - ma; What

e'er our lot, through storm or shot, Here's suc - cess to the Al - a - ba - ma! ba - ma!

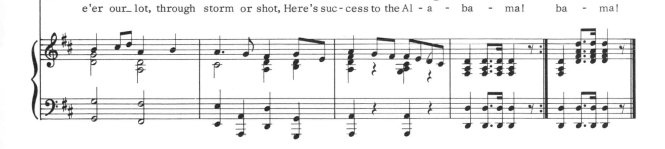

### 2.
Our country calls all hands to arms,
   We hear but to obey;
Nor shall home's most endearing charms
   Steal one weak thought away.
Our saucy craft shall roam the deep.
   We've sworn, lads, to defend her;
Trim, taut and tight, we'll brave the fight.
   Our motto, "No Surrender!"

*Chorus*: Then sling the bowl, etc.

### 3.

Our home is on the mountain wave,
  Our flag floats proudly free;
No boasting despot, tyrant, knave,
  Shall crush fair Liberty.
Firmly we'll aid her glorious cause,
  We'll die, boys, to defend her;
We'll brave the foe where'er we go,
  Our motto, "No Surrender!"

*Chorus*: Then sling the bowl, etc.

### 4.

Boys! if perchance it may befall,
  When storm of battle raves,
By shot or shell our noble hull
  Shall sink beneath the waves,
Yet while a plank to us is left
  To death we will defend her;
Facing the foe, down, down we'll go,
  But still cry, "No Surrender!"

*Chorus*: Then sling the bowl, etc.

# The *Alabama* and *Kearsarge*

Words and Music:
Frank Wilder

   The U.S.S. *Kearsarge,* captained by John A. Winslow of the Federal Navy, finally caught up with the *Alabama.* In June, 1864, while the *Alabama* was in Cherbourg harbor for repairs, she was challenged to battle by the *Kearsarge.* Captain Semmes accepted the challenge and the *Alabama* was sent to "Davy Jones' locker."

1. The Al - a - ba - ma's gone, hur - rah! To "Da - vy Jones - 's

Lock - er" far, There's noth - ing left of her to mar our com - merce on the

sea! The he - ro of "chro - nom - e - ters," Was van - quished by the

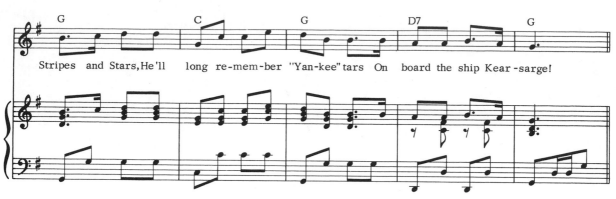

Stripes and Stars, He'll long re-mem-ber "Yan-kee" tars On board the ship Kear-sarge!

*Chorus*

The Al - a - ba - ma's gone, hur - rah! To "Da - vy Jones-'s Lock- er" far, There's

noth - ing left of her to mar Our com-merce on the sea! sea!

**2.**

The rebel pirate sought the fray,
    And for the Kearsarge bore away;
He thought to make a great display,
    And all of us astound!
He hail'd us with a full broadside,
    But yet no "yankee shot" replied
Until the gallant Captain cried,
    "Come lads! give them a round!"

*Chorus*: Then Alabama's gone, etc.

### 3.

Then came a sound that echoed far!
   With cheer on cheer from "Yankee tar!"
And sinking ship and trembling spar,
   A scene of death soon told!
Down to the bottom of the deep
   Sank many a traitor foe to sleep,
While Semmes the hero "like a sheep"
   Went to an English fold.

*Chorus*:  Then Alabama's gone, etc.

# For Bales

Words: A. E. Blackmar
Music: Patrick Sarsfield Gilmore

This is a Southern parody on "When Johnny Comes Marching Home" that was very popular in New Orleans between 1863 and 1864. The song tells how the Confederate Generals E. Kirby Smith and Richard Taylor "thwarted" the Union attempt to seize cotton stored up at Red River. The Federal government wanted to purchase the cotton, but this idea was not favored by the Union General, N. P. Banks. Hence the reference to Banks with a (?).

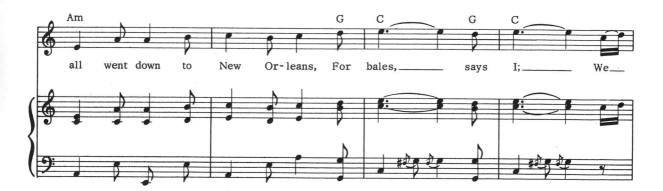

all   drink   stone   blind,   John-ny   fill   up   the   bowl."____   bowl."____

**2.**

We thought when we got in the "Ring,"
  For bales, for bales;
We thought when we got in the "Ring"
  For bales, says I;
We thought when we got in the "Ring,"
Greenbacks would be a dead sure thing,
"And we'll all drink stone blind,
  Johnny fill up the bowl."

**3.**

The "ring" went up, with bagging and rope,
  For bales, for bales;
Upon the "Black Hawk" with bagging and rope,
  For bales, says I;
Went up "Red River" with bagging and rope,
Expecting to make a pile of "soap,"
"And we'll all drink stone blind,
  Johnny fill up the bowl."

**4.**

But Taylor and Smith, with ragged ranks,
  For bales, for bales;
But Taylor and Smith, with ragged ranks,
  For bales, says I;
But Taylor and Smith, with ragged ranks,
Burned up the cotton and whipped old Banks,
"And we'll all drink stone blind,
  Johnny fill up the bowl."

**5.**

Our "ring" came back and cursed and swore,
  For bales, for bales;
Our "ring" came back and cursed and swore,
  For bales, says I;
Our "ring" came back and cursed and swore,
For we got no cotton at Grand Ecore,
"And we'll all drink stone blind,
  Johnny fill up the bowl."

**6.**

Now let us all give praise and thanks,
  For bales, for bales;
Now let us all give praise and thanks,
  For bales, says I;
Now let us all give praise and thanks
For the victory (?) gained by General Banks,
"And we'll all drink stone blind,
  Johnny fill up the bowl."

# Little Major

Words and Music:
Henry Clay Work

In a green field stained with crimson, the drummer boy lies forsaken. Only the Heavens look down and weep with teardrops of relief. This symbolic portrayal reveals man's anguish in war and God's everlasting mercy.

Tenderly

1. At his post the Lit - tle Ma - jor Dropp'd his drum that bat - tle-

day; On the grass all stain'd with crim - son Thro' that bat - tle-night he___

lay Cry-ing, "Oh! for love of Je - sus, Grant me but this lit - tle

boon! Can you, friend, re-fuse me wa - ter? Can you, when I die so soon?"

*Chorus*

Cry - ing, "Oh! for love of Je - sus, Grant me but this lit - tle boon! Can you,

friend, re-fuse me wa - ter? Can you, when I die so soon?" soon?"

**2.**

There are none to hear or help him —
All his friends were early fled,
Save the forms outstretch'd around him,
Of the dying and the dead.
Hush, they come! there falls a footstep!
How it makes his heart rejoice!
They will help, Oh, they will save him,
When they hear his fainting voice —

*Chorus*: Crying, "Oh, for love, etc.

**3.**

Now the lights are flashing round him,
    And he hears a loyal word,
Strangers they, whose lips pronounce it,
    Yet he trusts his voice is heard.
It is heard — Oh, God forgive them!
    They refuse his dying pray'r!
"Nothing but a wounded drummer,"
    So they say, and leave him there —

*Chorus:* Crying, "Oh, for love, etc.

**4.**

See! the moon that shone above him,
    Veils her face, as if in grief;
And the skies are sadly weeping —
    Shedding tear-drops of relief.
Yet to die, by friends forsaken,
    With his last request denied;
This he felt his keenest anguish,
    When at morn, he gasp'd and died —

*Chorus:* Crying, "Oh, for love, etc.

# All Quiet Along the Potomac Tonight

Words: Ethel Lynn Beers
Music: John Hill Hewitt

This song was popular with both armies. The title is derived from newspaper reports which were ribbing General McClellan's policy of delay after the first defeat of the Union forces at Bull Run, July 21, 1861. While the "Army of the Potomac" was being trained and organized, Lincoln's patience became strained and he wrote to McClellan:

"My dear McClellan: If you don't want to use the army, I should like to borrow it for a while. Yours respectfully, A. Lincoln."

The poem was published in Harper's Magazine in November, 1861, under the title "Picket Guard." The authorship of the poem was claimed by a famed cavalry leader, Major Lamar Fontaine, C.S.A. The composer of the music was born in New York and at the time of the war was one of the most popular song writers in the South.

1. All qui-et a-long the Po-to-mac to-night, Ex-cept here and there a stray pick-et Is shot, as he walks on his beat to and fro, By a ri-fle-man hid in the thick-et: 'Tis noth-ing, a pri-vate or

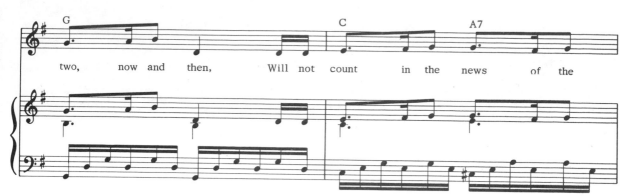

two, now and then, Will not count in the news of the

bat - tle: Not an of - fi - cer lost, on - ly one of the men, Moan-ing

out all a - lone the death rat - tle, All qui - et a -

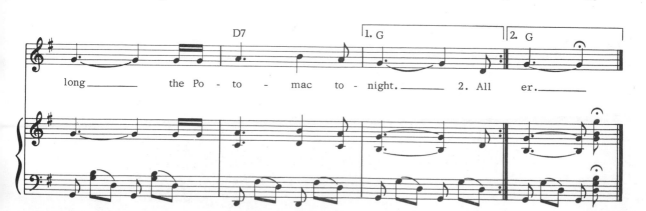

long＿＿＿ the Po - to - mac to - night.＿＿＿ 2. All er.＿＿＿

2.

"All quiet along the Potomac tonight,"
    Where the soldiers lie peacefully dreaming,
And their tents in the rays of the clear autumn moon,
    And the light of the camp fires are gleaming.
A tremulous sigh, as the gentle night wind
    Thro' the forest leaves slowly is creeping,
While the stars up above, with their glittering eyes,
    Keep guard o'er the army while sleeping.

3.

There's only the sound of the lone sentry's tread,
    As he tramps from the rock to the fountain,
And thinks of the two on the low trundle bed,
    Far away in the cot on the mountain.
His musket falls slack — his face, dark and grim,
    Grows gentle with memories tender,
As he mutters a prayer for the children asleep,
    And their mother — "may Heaven defend her."

4.

Then drawing his sleeve roughly over his eyes,
    He dashes off the tears that are welling;
And gathers his gun close up to his breast
    As if to keep down the heart's swelling.
He passes the fountain, the blasted pine tree,
    And his footstep is lagging and weary:
Yet onward he goes, thro' the broad belt of light,
    Towards the shades of the forest so dreary.

5.

Hark! was it the night wind that rustles the leaves?
    Was it the moonlight so wondrously flashing?
It looked like a rifle! "Ha! Mary, good-bye!"
    And his life-blood is ebbing and plashing.
"All quiet along the Potomac tonight,"
    No sound save the rush of the river;
While soft falls the dew on the face of the dead.
    "The Picket's" off duty forever.

INFANTRYMAN ON PICKET.

# The Drummer Boy of Shiloh

Words and Music:
Will Shakespeare Hays

This was one of the "big song hits" of the period. It inspired other composers to create songs about the drummer boys of Antietam, Gettysburg, Vicksburg and also imaginative ballads about their actions and role in the war. There were more than 100,000 boys in the war who were under sixteen years of age and of these there were drummer boys below the age of thirteen.

The battle near the old Shiloh Meeting House on the Tennessee River was one of the bitterest in the war. In this doleful ballad the dying confederate drummer boy prays, "while brave men knelt and cried."

1. On Shi - loh's dark and blood-y ground The dead and wound - ed

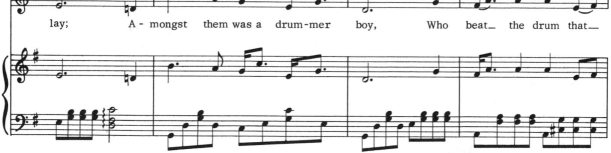

lay; A - mongst them was a drum-mer boy, Who beat— the drum that—

day. A wound - ed sol - dier held him up. His drum was by his

side; He clasp'd his hands,— then— rais'd his eyes, And

prayed— be-fore he died. He clasp'd his hands, then rais'd his

eyes, And prayed— be-fore he died. 2. Look died!

2.

"Look down upon the battle field,
 Oh, Thou, our Heavenly Friend!
Have mercy on our sinful souls!"
 The soldiers cried "A-men!"
For gathered 'round a little group,
 Each brave man knelt and cried;
They listened to the drummer boy,
 Who prayed before he died.
(Repeat last two lines)

3.

"Oh, mother," said the dying boy,
  "Look down from Heaven on me,
Receive me to thy fond embrace —
  Oh, take me home to thee.
I've loved my country as my God;
  To serve them both I've tried."
He smiled, shook hands — death seized the boy
  Who prayed before he died.
(Repeat last two lines)

4.

Each soldier wept, then, like a child —
  Stout hearts were they, and brave;
The flag his winding-sheet — God's Book
  The key unto his grave.
They wrote upon a simple board
  These words: "This is a guide
To those who'd mourn the drummer boy
  Who prayed before he died."
(Repeat last two lines)

5.

Ye angels 'round the Throne of Grace,
  Look down upon the braves,
Who fought and died on Shiloh's plain,
  Now slumb'ring in their graves!
How many homes made desolate —
  How many hearts have sighed —
How many, like that drummer boy,
  Who prayed before they died!
(Repeat last two lines)

THE DRUMMER.

THE FAVORITE IN CAMP

# Stonewall's Requiem

Words and Music:
M. Deeves

It was at Chancellorsville that Stonewall Jackson was accidentally shot by his own soldiers. "You have lost your left arm, while I have lost my right," wrote General Lee to the wounded general. Other complications set in and the great Stonewall "passed over the river" and was laid to rest "in the shade of the trees." This song commemorates his death and the great loss to the Confederacy.

Quite slow, with deep feeling

The muf-fled drum is beat-ing, There's a sad and sol-emn tread, Our

Ban-ner's draped in mourn-ing, As it shrouds th' illus-trious dead; Proud forms are bent with

sor-row, And all South-ern hearts are sore, The He-ro now is sleep-ing, No-ble

Stone-wall is no more, 'Mid the rat - tling of the mus-kets And the can - non's thun - d'rous

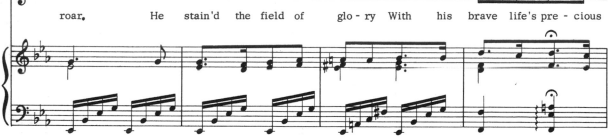

roar. He stain'd the field of glo - ry With his brave life's pre - cious

gore, And tho' our flag waved proud - ly, We were vic - tors ere sun - set, The

gal - lant deeds of Chance-lors-ville Will min - gle with re - gret. 2. They've love.

2.

They've borne him to an honor'd grave,
    The Laurel crown his brow,
By hallow'd James' silent wave
    He's sweetly sleeping now;
Virginia to the South is dear,
    She holds a sacred trust,
Our fallen braves from far and near,
    Are cover'd with her dust;
She shrines the spot where now is laid
    The bravest of them all,
The Martyr of our country's cause,
    Our Idoliz'd Stonewall;
But tho' his spirit's wafted
    To the happy realms above,
His name shall live forever link'd
    With reverence and love.

# Our Comrade Has Fallen

Words: W. T. Rossiter
Music: O. W. Brewster

This has been characterized as a "comrade gather around" song. A plaintive melody accompanies the fervent, patriotic lyric.

Slowly, with deep expression

Our com-rade has fall - en, He's gone to his rest, His_ voice in full

cho - rus Now joins with the blest, O, weep for the fall - en! No

more shall we hear His tones in sweet mu - sic Fall soft on the ear.

**2.**

The flag of our country,
   'Mid cannon's deep roar,
Where fierce raged the battle,
   Still proudly he bore.
The stars and the stripes now
   Float over his grave;
He died for his country,
   His country to save.

*Chorus*: Tread lightly, etc.

**3.**

Our comrade has fallen,
   He's gone to his home;
That bright world of glory,
   Where blest spirits roam;
O weep for the fallen!
   We'll see him no more,
Till we join the chorus
   On Canaan's fair shore.

*Chorus*: Tread lightly, etc.

208

# 'Twas at the Siege of Vicksburg

Words: Anonymous
Music: Septimus Winner

The Confederates adapted this catchy tune by a Northern composer to describe the bombardment of the strategic port city. The "Minnie balls" and "Parrot shells" were coming from General David Porter's Union fleet.

The original title of the tune is "Listen to the Mocking Bird." Sep. Winner used the pen name of Alice Hawthorne in the first printing of this song.

2.

Oh, well will we remember,
Remember, remember,
Tough mule meat, June sans November;
And the minnie-balls that whistled through the air —

*Chorus*:

    Listen to the minnie-balls,
    Listen to the minnie-balls,
    The minnie-balls are singing in the air.
    (Repeat last three lines)

# A Life on the Vicksburg Bluff

Words: A. Dalsheimer
Music: "A Life On The Ocean Wave"
     by Henry Russell

Henry Russell was an Englishman who lived in America from 1833 to 1841. He was a very successful song writer and this tune, composed in 1838, was one of the most popular pieces before and during the war.

The writer of the lyric was a member of the Third Louisiana Regiment during the siege. The song vividly and humorously describes the hardships of the famished garrison and the pandemonium caused by the incessant bombardment. General John C. Pemberton surrendered to Grant on July 4, 1863.

Moderato

1. A life on the Vicks-burg bluff,____ A ____ home in the trench-es deep,____ Where we dodge "Yank" shells e-nough,____ And our old "pea-bread" won't keep.____ On "old Lo-gan's" beef I pine,____ For there's fat on his bones no

more;____ Oh! give me some pork and brine,____ And truck from a sut-lers store.____ A

life on the Vicks-burg bluff,____ A___ home in the trench-es deep,____ When we

dodge "Yank" shells e-nough,____ And our old pea-bread_won't keep,____ Pea-

bread,____ pea-bread____ Our old pea-bread won't keep,____ Pea-

bread,_____ pea - bread,_____ Our old pea-bread won't keep._____ keep._____

2.

Old Grant is starving us out,
　Our grub is fast wasting away,
Pemb' don't know what he's about,
　And he hasn't for many a day,
So we'll bury "old Logan" tonight,
　From tough beef we'll be set free;
We'll put him far out of sight,
　No more of his meat for me.
A life on the Vicksburg bluff, etc.

3.

Texas steers are no longer in view,
　Mule steaks are now "done up brown,"
While peabread, mule roast and mule stew,
　Are our fare in Vicksburg town;
And the song of our hearts shall be,
　While the Yanks and their gunboats rave;
A life in a bomb-proof for me,
　And a tear on "old Logan's" grave.
A life on the Vicksburg bluff, etc.

# Hold the Fort

Words and Music:
P. P. Bliss

In the 1880 edition of this song, the incident upon which it is based was recorded by a Major Whittle. During October, 1864, a strategic position at Altoona Pass was being held by General Corse of Illinois. The Union Garrison was outnumbered and surrounded, and the Confederate General French summoned the Yankees to surrender. When Corse refused, fierce fighting ensued, and he was forced to the crest of the hill. The situation seemed hopeless, until a Union officer caught sight of a signal flag across the valley atop Kenesaw Mountain. The signal was answered, and soon the message was waved from mountain to mountain "Hold the fort for I am coming W. T. Sherman." Cheers went up and, under murderous fire, the position was held. Within three hours, Sherman's advanced guard had forced the Confederates to retreat.

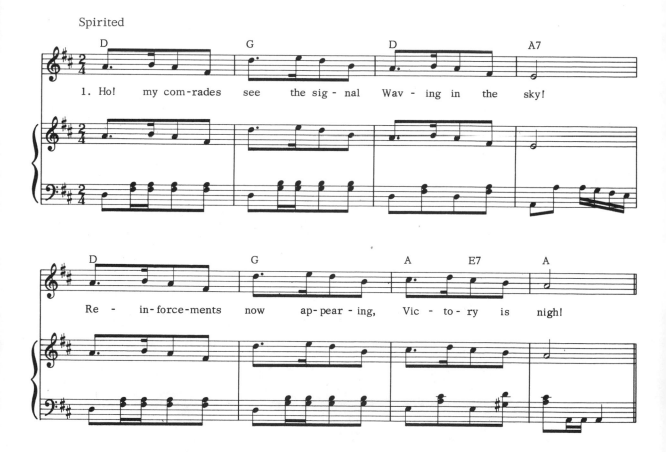

*Chorus*

"Hold the fort, for I am com - ing," Je - sus sig - nals still,

Wave the an - swer back to heav - en, "By thy grace, we will." will."

2.
See the mighty host advancing,
  Satan leading on;
Mighty men around us falling,
  Courage almost gone.

*Chorus*: "Hold the fort, etc.

3.
See the glorious banner waving,
  Hear the bugle blow;
In our Leader's name we'll triumph
  Over ev'ry foe.

*Chorus*: "Hold the fort, etc.

4.
Fierce and long the battle rages,
  But our Help is near;
Onward comes our Great Commander,
  Cheer, my comrades, cheer!

*Chorus*: "Hold the fort, etc.

# When Sherman Marched down to the Sea

Words: Lt. S. H. M. Byers
Music: "Old Rosin the Beau"

While confined in the Rebel Prison camp at Columbia, South Carolina, Adjutant Byers of the Fifth Iowa Infantry composed this song. Herded together with several hundred other officers, suffering from cold and hunger, his spirit was unbroken because he was able to get and read true accounts, via secret methods, of Sherman's victorious march to the sea. It is reported that when Sherman took Columbia, he made contact with the author and sent him North. A million copies of the song were sold by 1866. Many publishers stole the words and set them to various tunes. Adjutant Byers received five dollars in royalties from the original publisher. Sigmund Spaeth notes that the tune was used for at least four political songs between 1840 and 1875.

The tune and original lyric was a Southern favorite although its source is still a riddle. The melody has a Scotch or Irish flavor. The word "Beau" is also spelled "Bow" and may have referred to a minstrel fiddler. And as Sigmund Spaeth put it, "there is nothing to prove that "Old Rosin" was anything more than a ladies' man with alcoholic tendencies.*

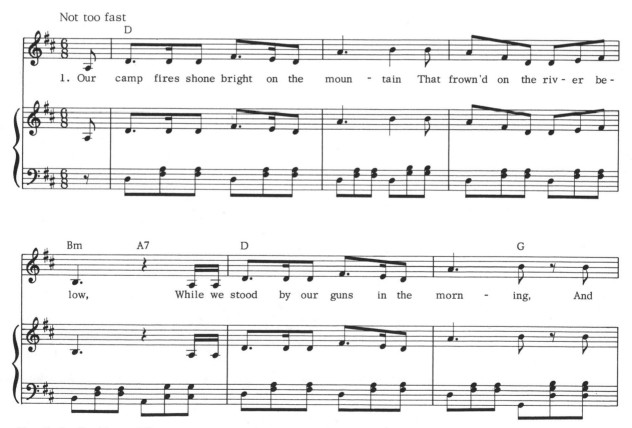

1. Our camp fires shone bright on the moun - tain That frown'd on the riv - er below, While we stood by our guns in the morn - ing, And

*Spaeth, S., *Read 'em and Weep*

ea - ger - ly watch'd for the foe;\_\_\_\_\_ When a horse-man rode out from the

dark - ness That hung o - ver moun - tain and tree, And

shout - ed, "Boys, up and be read - y, For Sher-man will march to the sea."\_\_\_\_\_

2.

When cheer upon cheer for bold Sherman
Went up from each valley and glen,
And the bugles re-echoed the music
That came from the lips of the men —
For we knew that the stars on our banners,
More bright in their splendor would be
And the blessings from Northland would greet us
When Sherman march'd down to the sea.

GENERAL WILLIAM T. SHERMAN AT ATLANTA.
From a photograph.

3.

Then forward, boys; forward to battle,
　　We march'd on our wearysome way,
And we storm'd the wild hills of Resaca,
　　God bless those who fell on that day! —
Then Kenesaw, dark in its glory,
　　Frown'd down on the flag of the free,
But the East and the West bore her standard
　　When Sherman march'd down to the sea.

4.

Still onward we pressed till our banners
　　Swept out from Atlanta's grim walls,
And the blood of the patriot dampened
　　The soil where the traitor's flag falls;
But we paused not to weep for the fallen
　　Who slept by each river and tree,
Yet we twined them a wreath of the laurel,
　　And Sherman march'd down to the sea.

5.

Proud, proud was our army that morning
　　That stood by the cypress and pine,
Then Sherman said, "Boys, you are weary,
　　This day fair Savannah is mine!"
Then sang we a song for our chieftain,
　　That echoed o'er river and sea
And the stars on our banners shone brighter
　　When Sherman march'd down to the sea.

# We are marching
## on to Richmond

# We Are Marching on to Richmond

Words and Music:
E. W. Locke

General Grant took command of all Union forces in March, 1864. On April 3, 1865, after bitter fighting and great loss of life, besieged and burning Richmond was captured. This strategic victory spelled the doom of the Confederacy.

Our knap-sacks sling, and blithe - ly sing, We're march-ing on to Rich-mond; With

weap-ons bright, and hearts so light, We're march - ing on to Rich-mond. Each

wear - y mile with song be - guile, We're march - ing on to Rich-mond; The

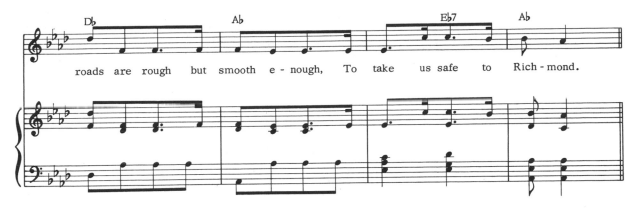

roads are rough but smooth e - nough, To take us safe to Rich - mond.

*Chorus*

Then tramp a - way while the bu - gles play, We're march - ing on to Rich - mond; Our

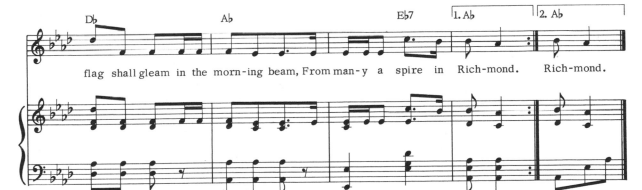

flag shall gleam in the morn - ing beam, From man - y a spire in Rich - mond. Rich - mond.

### 2.

Our foes are near, their drums we hear,
    They're camped about in Richmond;
With pickets out, to tell the route,
    Our army takes to Richmond.
We've crafty foes to meet our blows,
    No doubt they'll fight for Richmond;
The brave may die but never fly,
    We'll cut our way to Richmond.

*Chorus*: Then tramp away, etc.

### 3.

But yesterday, in murd'rous fray,
   While marching on to Richmond,
We parted here from comrades dear,
   While marching on to Richmond;
With manly sighs and tearful eyes,
   While marching on to Richmond,
We laid the braves in peaceful graves,
   And started on for Richmond.

*Chorus*: Then tramp away, etc.

### 4.

Our friends away are sad today,
   Because we march to Richmond;
With loving fears they shrink to hear,
   About our march to Richmond;
The pen shall tell that they who fell,
   While marching on to Richmond,
Had hearts aglow and face to foe
   While marching on to Richmond.

*Chorus*: Then tramp away, etc.

### 5.

Our thoughts shall roam to scenes of home
   While marching on to Richmond.
The vacant chair that's waiting there
   While we march on to Richmond;
'Twill not be long till shout and song
   We'll raise aloud in Richmond,
And war's rude blast, will soon be past,
   And we'll go home from Richmond.

*Chorus*: Then tramp away, etc.

# Marching Through Georgia

Words and Music:
Henry Clay Work

This song tells of the spirit of the Union soldiers on the march, the jubilation of the Negroes greeting Sherman's Army, the cheers of the freed Union prisoners of war, and finally, it hails the triumph of the march to the sea. Although this spirited song was one of the war's most popular, it represents only one side of the coin. It must be remembered that the destruction wreaked by Sherman's troops was terrifying.

Carl Sandburg writes:

"Over many square miles of this area now was left not a chicken, not a pig, nor horse, nor cow, nor sheep, not a smokehouse ham nor side of bacon. . .not a mule to plow land with, not a piece of railroad track. . ..
War as a reality, a pervasive stench of conquest, had come to Georgia."*

1. Bring the good old bu-gle, boys, we'll sing an-oth-er song, Sing it with a spir-it that will start the world a-long, Sing it as we used to sing it, fif-ty thou-sand strong, While we were march-ing through Geor-gia.

*Carl Sandburg, *Storm Over The Land*
Harcourt Brace, 1942, p. 335

*Chorus*

Hur - rah! Hur-rah! we bring the ju - bi - lee! Hur - rah! Hur-rah! the

flag that makes you free! So we sang the cho-rus from At - lan - ta to the sea,

While we were march - ing through Geor - gia. Geor - gia.

**2.**
How the darkeys shouted
When they heard the joyful sound!
How the turkeys gobbled
Which our commissary found!
How the sweet potatoes
Even started from the ground,
While we were marching through Georgia.

*Chorus*: Hurrah! Hurrah! etc.

### 3.

Yes, and there were Union men
Who wept with joyful tears,
When they saw the honor'd flag
They had not seen for years;
Hardly could they be restrained
From breaking forth in cheers,
While we were marching through Georgia.

*Chorus*: Hurrah! Hurrah! etc.

### 4.

"Sherman's dashing Yankee boys
Will never reach the coast!"
So the saucy rebels said,
And 'twas a handsome boast;
Had they not forgot, alas!
To reckon with the host,
While we were marching through Georgia.

*Chorus*: Hurrah! Hurrah! etc.

### 5.

So we made a thoroughfare
For Freedom and her train,
Sixty miles in latitude —
Three hundred to the main;
Treason fled before us,
For resistance was in vain,
While we were marching through Georgia.

*Chorus*: Hurrah! Hurrah! etc.

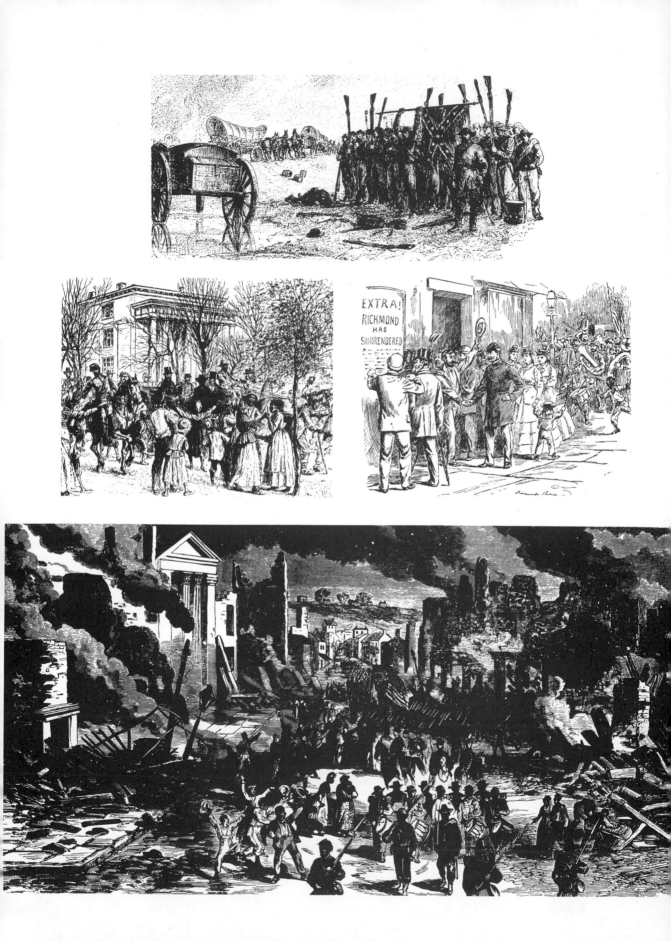

# Part Four

# Somebody's Darling

# Somebody's Darling

Words: Marie Revenel De La Coste
Music: John Hill Hewitt

These words were set to many different tunes, but it was John Hill Hewitt's melody which gained the most popularity in the South. Harwell reminds us, in his *Songs of the Confederacy,* that it "will be remembered by many for Margaret Mitchell's effective use of it in *Gone With The Wind."*

Slowly, with feeling

In - to the ward of the clean, white-wash'd halls Where the dead slept and the dy - ing lay, Wound - ed by bay - o - nets, sa - bres and balls, Some - bod - y's dar - ling was borne one day. Some - bod - y's dar - ling, so

young and so brave, Wear-ing still on his sweet, yet pale face,

Soon to be hid in the dust of the grave, The lin-ger-ing light of his

*Chorus*

boy - hood's grace. Some-bod - y's dar - ling, Some-bod - y's pride,

Who'll tell his moth - er where her boy__ died. where her boy__ died.

### 2.

Matted and damp are his tresses of gold,
Kissing the snow of that fair young brow;
Pale are the lips of most delicate mould,
Somebody's darling is dying now.
Back from his beautiful purple vein'd brow
Brush off the wand'ring waves of gold;
Cross his white hands on his broad bosom now,
Somebody's darling is still and cold.

*Chorus*:  Somebody's darling, etc.

### 3.

Give him a kiss, but for Somebody's sake,
Murmur a pray'r for him, soft and low;
One little curl from its golden mates take,
Somebody's pride they were once, you know;
Somebody's warm hand has oft rested there,
Was it a mother's so soft and white?
Or have the lips of a sister, so fair,
Ever been bath'd in their waves of light?

*Chorus*:  Somebody's darling, etc.

### 4.

Somebody's watching and waiting for him,
Yearning to hold him again to her breast;
Yet, there he lies with his blue eyes so dim.
And purple, child-like lips half apart.
Tenderly bury the fair, unknown dead,
Pausing to drop on his grave a tear;
Carve on the wooden slab over his head,
Somebody's darling is slumbering here.

*Chorus*:  Somebody's darling, etc.

# Lorena

Words: Rev. H. D. L. Webster
Music: J. P. Webster

Here is the "Annie Laurie" of the Confederate Armies. In *Pen and Ink* Brander Matthews says, "this doleful old ditty started at the start and never stopped until the last musket was stacked and the last camp fire cold." It was the song nearest to the Confederate soldier's heart.

"Maggie Howell (the sister-in-law of President Jefferson Davis), says there is a girl in large hoops and a calico frock at every piano between Richmond and Mississippi, banging on the out of tune thing and looking up into a man's face, singing that song. The man wears a soiled and battle stained uniform, but his heart is fresh enough, as he hangs over her, to believe in Lorena."*

Slowly, with much expression

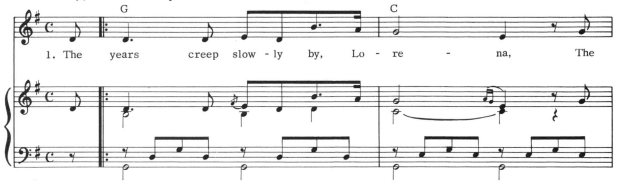

1. The years creep slow-ly by, Lo - re - na, The

snow is on the grass a - gain; The sun's low down the sky, Lo-

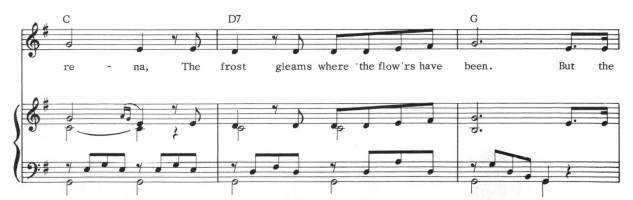

re - na, The frost gleams where the flow'rs have been. But the

*Mary Boykin Chestnut, *A Diary From Dixie* (Edited by B. A. Williams) p. 304
Houghton Mifflin Co.

heart throbs on as warm - ly now, As when the sum-mer days were

nigh; Oh! the sun can nev-er dip so low, _____ A -

down af - fec-tion's cloud-less sky. The sun can nev-er slip so

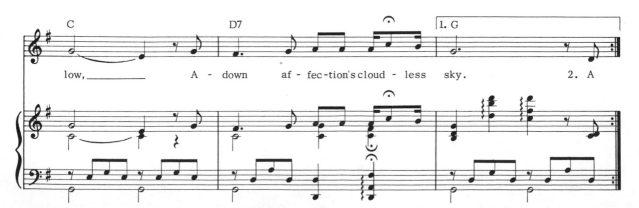

low, _____ A - down af - fec-tion's cloud - less sky. 2. A

heart.

### 2.

A hundred months have passed, Lorena,
  Since last I held that hand in mine,
And felt the pulse beat fast, Lorena,
  Though mine beat faster far than thine.
A hundred months, 'twas flowery May,
  When up the hilly slope we climbed,
To watch the dying of the day,
  And hear the distant church bells chime.
To watch the dying of the day,
  And hear the distant church bells chime.

### 3.

We loved each other then, Lorena,
  More than we ever dared to tell;
And what we might have been, Lorena,
  Had but our lovings prospered well —
But then, 'tis past, the years are gone,
  I'll not call up their shadowy forms;
I'll say to them, "Lost years, sleep on!
  Sleep on! nor heed life's pelting storms."
I'll say to them, "Lost years, sleep on!
  Sleep on! nor heed life's pelting storms."

### 4.

The story of that past, Lorena,
  Alas! I care not to repeat,
The hopes that could not last, Lorena,
  They lived, but only lived to cheat.
I would not cause e'en one regret
  To rankle in your bosom now;
For "If we try, we may forget,"
  Were words of thine long years ago.
For "If we try, we may forget,"
  Were words of thine long years ago.

### 5.

Yes, these were words of thine, Lorena,
  They burn within my memory yet;
They touched some tender chords, Lorena,
  Which thrill and tremble with regret.
'Twas not thy woman's heart that spoke;
  Thy heart was always true to me:
A duty, stern and pressing, broke
  The tie which linked my soul with thee.
A duty, stern and pressing, broke
  The tie which linked my soul with thee.

### 6.

It matters little now, Lorena,
  The past is in the eternal past,
Our heads will soon lie low, Lorena,
  Life's tide is ebbing out so fast.
There is a Future! O, thank God!
  Of life this is so small a part!
'Tis dust to dust beneath the sod!
  But there, up there, 'tis heart to heart.
'Tis dust to dust beneath the sod!
  But there, up there, 'tis heart to heart.

# Aura Lea

Words: W. W. Fosdick, Esq.
Music: G. R. Poulton

Without the tradition of our "shape note" hymns, this beautiful melody could not have been written. Here is that unique fusion of hymn and spiritual which created that distinctive 19th century American flavor. In the present revival of folk music, Aura Lee has become very popular under the title of "Love Me Tender."

Slowly, with feeling

1. When the Black-bird in the Spring, On the wil - low tree

Sat and rock'd, I heard him sing, sing - ing Au - ra Lea.

Au - ra Lea, Au - ra Lea, Maid of gold - en hair;

Sun - shine came a - long with thee, And swal - lows in the air.

*Chorus*

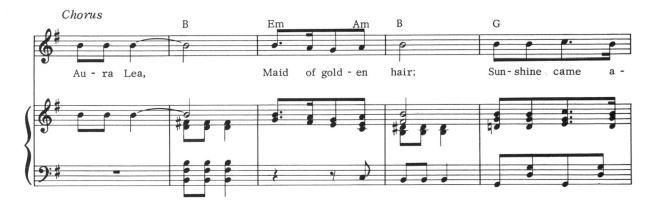

Au - ra Lea, Maid of gold - en hair; Sun - shine came a -

long with thee, And swal - lows in the air. air.

**2.**
In thy blush the rose was born,
  Music when you spake,
Through thine azure eye the morn,
  Sparkling seemed to break.
Aura Lea, Aura Lea,
  Birds of crimson wing,
Never song have sung to me
  As in that sweet spring.

*Chorus*: Aura Lea, Aura Lea, etc.

**3.**
Aura Lea! the bird may flee,
  The willow's golden hair
Swing through winter fitfully,
  On the stormy air.
Yet if thy blue eyes I see,
  Gloom will soon depart;
For to me, sweet Aura Lea
  Is sunshine through the heart.

*Chorus*: Aura Lea, Aura Lea, etc.

**4.**
When the mistletoe was green,
  Midst the winter's snows,
Sunshine in thy face was seen,
  Kissing lips of rose.
Aura Lea, Aura Lea,
  Take my golden ring;
Love and light return with thee,
  And swallows with the spring.

*Chorus*: Aura Lea, Aura Lea, etc.

# Just Before the Battle, Mother

Words and Music:
George F. Root

This song was very popular with both armies. Many of the soldiers were young and far away from home for the first time. Hence, the theme of "Mother," "Father" and "Brother" appears as titles for numerous songs.

well they know that on the mor-row, Some will sleep be-neath the sod.

*Chorus*

Fare-well, Moth-er, you may nev-er_____ Press me to your heart a - gain; But

O, you'll not for-get me, Moth-er, If I'm num-ber'd with the slain. slain.

2.
Oh, I long to see you, Mother,
  And the loving ones at home,
But I'll never leave our banner
  Till in honor I can come.
Tell the traitors, all around you,
  That their cruel words, we know,
In ev'ry battle kill our soldiers
  By the help they give the foe.

*Chorus*: Farewell, Mother, etc.

3.
Hark! I hear the bugles sounding,
  'Tis the signal for the fight,
Now may God protect us, Mother,
  As He ever does the right.
Hear the "Battle Cry of Freedom."
  How it swells upon the air,
Oh, yes we'll rally round the standard
  Or we'll perish nobly there.

*Chorus*: Farewell, Mother, etc.

# Never Forget the Dear Ones

## A Home Song

Words and Music:
George F. Root

This song brings a message from home to the soldier who is far away in the field of battle. It pleads that he never forget the home folks, for their love is with him and awaits him back home.

**2.**

Ever their hearts are turning
    To thee when far away,
Their love so pure and tender,
    Is with thee on thy way;
Where ever thou may'st wander
    Where ever thou may'st roam,
Never forget the dear ones
    That cluster round thy home,
Never forget, never forget,
    Never forget the dear ones,
That cluster round thy home.

*Chorus*: Never forget, etc.

**3.**

Never forget thy Father,
    Who cheerful toils for thee,
Within thy heart may ever
    Thy mother's image be;
Thy sister dear and brother
    They long for thee to come,
Never forget the dear ones
    That cluster round thy home,
Never forget, never forget,
    Never forget the dear ones,
That cluster round thy home.

*Chorus*: Never forget, etc.

OFF TO THE WAR.

HOME AGAIN:

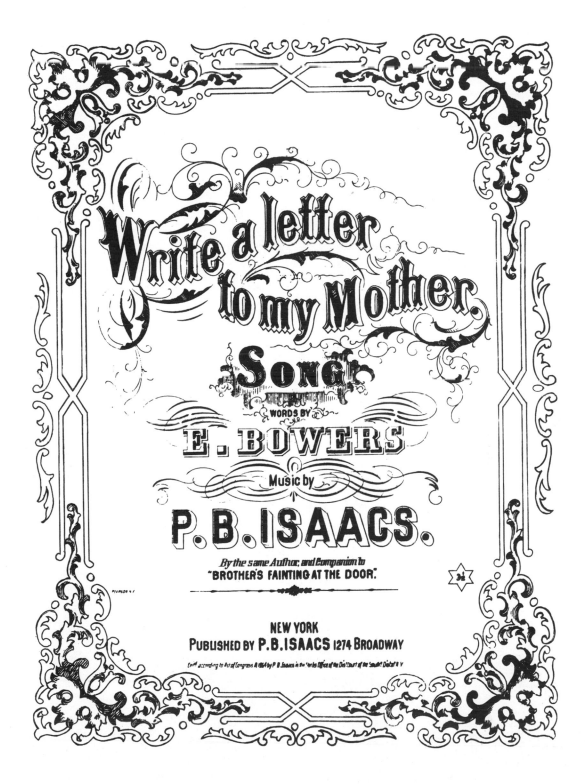

Write a letter to my Mother

Song

WORDS BY

E. BOWERS

Music by

P. B. ISAACS.

*By the same Author, and Companion to*
"BROTHER'S FAINTING AT THE DOOR".

NEW YORK

Published by P. B. ISAACS 1274 Broadway

Entd according to Act of Congress A 1864 by P. B. Isaacs in the Clerks Office of the Dist Court of the South. Dist of N Y

# Write a Letter to My Mother

Words: E. Bowers
Music: P. B. Isaacs

In this song an actual incident is recorded. A captured officer at the battle of Bull Run relates the following:

"I observed a Federal prisoner tenderly cared for by a Rebel Soldier. I gleaned from their conversation that they were brothers. . . .The dying boy with a smile of holy resignation clasped his brother's hand, spoke of their Father who was fighting for the dear old Flag, of Mother, of home, of childhood; then, requesting his brother to write a letter to Mother, and imploring him never to divulge the secret of his death, the young hero yielded up his life."

Slowly, with feeling

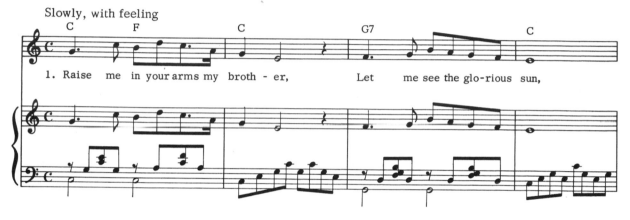

1. Raise me in your arms my broth - er, Let me see the glo-rious sun,

I am wear-y faint and dy - ing, How is the bat -tle, lost or won;

I re-mem-ber you my broth - er Sent to__ me that fa - tal dart.

Broth - er fight-ing a-gainst broth - er, 'Tis well, 'tis well that thus we part,

Broth - er fight-ing a-gainst broth - er, 'Tis well, 'tis well that thus we part.

*Chorus*

Write a let-ter to my moth-er, Send it when her boy is dead;

That he per-ish'd by his broth-er, Not a word of that be said. said.

2.

Father's fighting for the Union,
　And you may meet him on the field,
Could you raise your arm to smite him,
　Oh, could you bid that Father yield;
He who lov'd us in our childhood,
　Taught the infant pray'rs we said.
Brother take from me a warning,
　I'll soon be number'd with the dead.
Brother take from me a warning,
　I'll soon be number'd with the dead.

*Chorus*:　Write a letter, etc.

3.

Do you ever think of mother,
　In our home within the glen
Watching, praying for her children,
　Oh, would you see that home again;
Brother I am surely dying,
　Keep the secret for 'tis one
That would kill our angel mother,
　If she but knew what you have done.
That would kill our angel mother,
　If she but knew what you have done.

*Chorus*:　Write a letter, etc.

WRITING HOME

# The Yellow Rose of Texas

Words and Music:
Anonymous

This popular Confederate song was an offspring of the Minstrel stage. Its catchy tune was used for parody by both sides. After General Hood's disastrous campaign in Tennessee in 1864, the soldiers sang:

"And now I'm going Southward, for my heart is full of woe,
I'm going back to Georgia, to find my Uncle Joe.
You may talk about your dearest May, and sing of Rosalie,
But the gallant Hood of Texas, played hell in Tennessee."

1. There's a yel-low rose of Tex-as, that I am going to see, No oth-er dark-ey knows her, no dark-ey on-ly me; She cried so when I left her it like to broke my heart, And

if I ev - er find her, we nev - er more will part.

*Chorus*

She's the sweet - est rose of col - or this dark - ey ev - er knew, Her

eyes are bright as dia - monds, they spar - kle like the dew; You may

talk a - bout your Dear - est May, and sing of Ro - sa Lee, But the

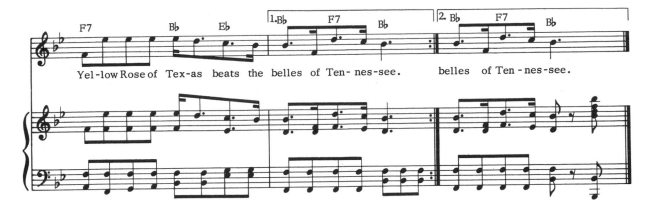

Yel-low Rose of Tex-as beats the belles of Ten- nes-see.    belles  of Ten -nes-see.

2.

Where the Rio Grande is flowing,
And the starry skies are bright,
She walks along the river
In the quiet summer night;
She thinks if I remember,
When we parted long ago,
I promised to come back again,
And not to leave her so.

*Chorus*:  She's the sweetest, etc.

3.

Oh now I'm going to find her,
For my heart is full of woe,
And we'll sing the song together
That we sang so long ago;
We'll play the banjo gaily,
And we'll sing the songs of yore,
And the Yellow Rose of Texas
Shall be mine for ever more.

*Chorus*:  She's the sweetest, etc.

# The Southern Girl

### or
### The Homespun Dress

Words: Carrie Bell Sinclair
Music: "The Irish Jaunting Car"

This song had wide circulation in the South and became part of our oral tradition. The weary years of war brought many hardships to the South, and old spinning wheels and looms were used by women to weave thread into cloth. To the same tune that was adopted for "The Bonnie Blue Flag," the young belle sings with pride and joy about her new dress made from "homespun" yarn.

With spirit

1. Oh, yes I am a South-ern girl, And glo-ry in the name,_____ And boast it with far great-er pride Than glit-t'ring wealth or fame;_____ I en-vy not the North-ern girl Her robes of beau-ty rare,_____ Tho'

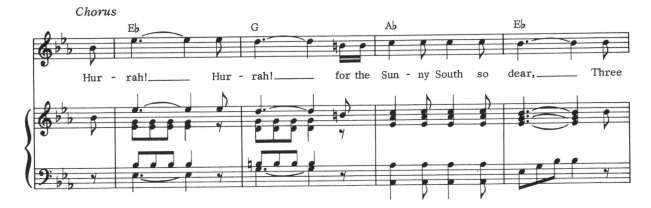

**Chorus**

**2.**
My homespun dress is plain, I know,
My hat's palmetto too,
But then it shows what Southern girls
For Southern rights will do;
We've sent the bravest of our land
To battle with the foe,
And we will lend a helping hand;
We love the South, you know.

*Chorus:* Hurrah! Hurrah! etc.

3.

The Southern land's a glorious land,
   And has a glorious cause,
Three cheers, three cheers for Southern Rights,
   And for the Southern Boys!
We've sent our sweethearts to the war,
   But dear girls, never mind,
Your soldier-boy will ne'er forget,
   The girl he left behind.

*Chorus*: Hurrah! Hurrah! etc.

4.

The soldier is the lad for me,
   A brave heart I adore;
And when the Sunny South is free,
   And fighting is no more,
I'll choose me then a lover brave
   From out that gallant band;
The soldier lad I love the best
   Shall have my heart and hand.

*Chorus*: Hurrah! Hurrah! etc.

5.

And now, young man, a word to you.
   If you would win the fair,
Go to the field where honor calls,
   And win your lady there.
Remember that our brightest smiles
   Are for the true and brave,
And that our tears are all for those
   Who fill a soldier's grave.

*Chorus*: Hurrah! Hurrah! etc.

# THE SOUTHERN SOLDIER BOY

Song,

As Sung by

## Miss Sallie Partington

IN THE

## VIRGINIA CAVALIER

AT THE

## Richmond New Theatre.

WORDS BY CAPT<sup>N</sup> C. W. ALEXANDER A.A.C & A.P.M

THE AIR THE BOY WITH THE AUBURN HAIR

Entered According to Act of Congress in the Year 1863, by George Dunn in the Clerk's Office of the District Court of the Confederate States of America, for the Eastern District of Virginia.

Richmond Va Lithog<sup>d</sup> & Published by Geo Dunn & Comp<sup>y</sup> P.O Box.991 Columbia S.C Julian A. Selby

# The Southern Soldier Boy

Words: Capt. G. W. Alexander
Music: "Boy With The Auburn Hair"

In this lilting melody the wife sings that she will be loving and dutiful when her soldier boy comes home. She has faith in the cause and looks forward to embracing her Southern Soldier Boy again. The tune has an Irish flavor, and has the seeds of that Northern song, "When Johnny Comes Marching Home."

fy; He is the dar-ling of my heart, My south-ern sol-dier boy. Yo!

**Chorus**

ho!____ yo! ho!____ yo! ho ho ho ho ho ho ho! ho!____ He is my on - ly

joy, He is the dar-ling of my heart, My south-ern sol-dier boy. boy.____

2.

When Bob comes home from war's alarms,
  We'll start anew in life,
I'll give myself right up to him,
  A dutiful, loving wife.
I'll try my best to please my dear,
  For he is my only joy;
He is the darling of my heart,
  My Southern Soldier Boy.

*Chorus*:
    Yo! ho! yo! ho! yo! ho! ho! ho!
        ho! ho! ho! ho!
    He is my only joy,
    He is the darling of my heart,
    My Southern Soldier Boy.

3.

Oh! if in battle he was slain,
　　I am sure that I should die,
But I am sure he'll come again
　　And cheer my weeping eye;
But should he fall in this our glorious cause,
　　He still would be my joy,
For many a sweetheart mourns the loss
　　Of a Southern Soldier Boy.

*Chorus*:

　　Yo! ho! yo! ho! yo! ho! ho! ho!
　　　　ho! ho! ho! ho!
　　I'd grieve to lose my joy,
　　But many a sweetheart mourns the loss
　　Of a Southern Soldier Boy.

4.

I hope for the best, and so do all
　　Whose hopes are in the field;
I know that we shall win the day,
　　For Southrons never yield,
And when we think of those that are away,
　　We'll look above for joy,
And I'm mighty glad that my Bobby is
　　A Southern Soldier Boy.

*Chorus*:

　　Yo! ho! yo! ho! yo! ho! ho! ho!
　　　　ho! ho! ho! ho!
　　He is my only joy,
　　He is the darling of my heart,
　　My Southern Soldier Boy.

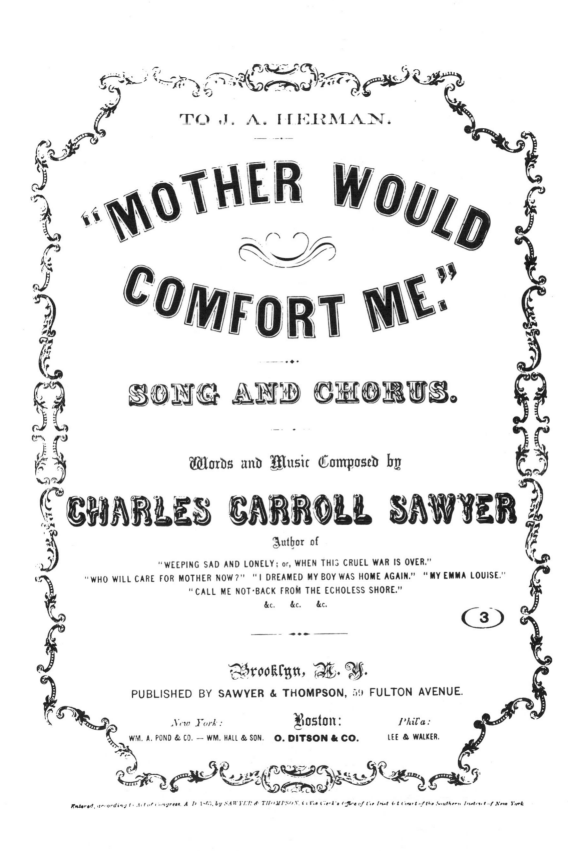

# Mother Would Comfort Me

Words and Music:
Charles Carroll Sawyer

The sentimental ballads by Charles C. Sawyer were favorites with both the North and the South. The 1868 edition of this song records the incident upon which it is based. A soldier from one of the New York regiments was severely wounded and taken prisoner. While in the hospital, he was told by the attendant that no more could be done for him, and he must die. His last words were the title to this song.

Slowly, with feeling

1. Wound - ed and sor - row - ful, far from my home, Sick a - mong stran - gers, un - cared for, un - known; E - ven the birds that used sweet - ly to sing Are si - lent, and swift - ly have tak - en the wing.

No one but Moth - er can cheer me to - day, No one for

me could so fer - vent - ly pray: None to con - sole me, no

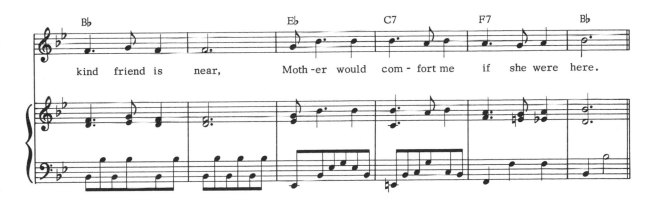

kind friend is near, Moth - er would com - fort me if she were here.

### Chorus

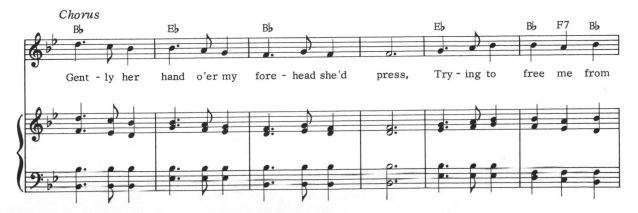

Gent - ly her hand o'er my fore - head she'd press, Try - ing to free me from

pain and dis - tress; Kind - ly she'd say to me, "Be of good

cheer, Moth - er will com - fort you, Moth - er is here!" here!"

**2.**

If she were with me, I soon would forget
My pain and my sorrow, no more would I fret;
One kiss from her lips, or one look from her eye,
Would make me contented, and willing to die!
Gently her hand o'er my forehead she'd press,
Trying to free me from pain and distress;
Kindly she'd say to me, "Be of good cheer,
Mother will comfort you, Mother is here!"

*Chorus*: Gently her hand, etc.

**3.**

Cheerfully, faithfully, Mother would stay
Always beside me, by night and by day;
If I should murmur or wish to complain,
Her gentle voice would soon calm me again.
Sweetly a Mother's love shines like a star,
Brightest in darkness, when daylight's afar;
In clouds or in sunshine, pleasures or pain,
Mother's affection is ever the same.

*Chorus*: Gently her hand, etc.

# Who Will Care for Mother Now?

Words and Music:
Charles Carroll Sawyer

The following is taken from the recorded data on the first edition:

> "The dying soldier was the sole support of an aged and sick mother for many years. Hearing the surgeon tell those around him that he could not live, he placed his hand across his forehead, and with a trembling voice said, while burning tears ran down his fevered cheeks: 'Who will take care of mother now?'"

260

an - swer; To my fate I meek-ly bow_____ If you'll

on - ly tell me tru - ly, Who will care for moth - er now?_____

*Chorus*

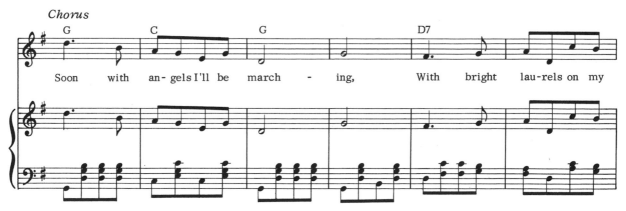

Soon with an-gels I'll be march - ing, With bright lau-rels on my

brow._____ I have for my coun-try fall - en.

Who will care for moth-er now?_____ now?_____

2.

Who will comfort her in sorrow?
　Who will dry the falling tear,
Gently smooth her wrinkled forehead?
　Who will whisper words of cheer?
Even now I think I see her
　Kneeling, praying for me! how
Can I leave her in her anguish?
　Who will care for mother now?

*Chorus*:  Soon with angels, etc.

3.

Let this knapsack be my pillow,
　And my mantle be the sky;
Hasten, comrades, to the battle,
　I will like a soldier die.
Soon with angels I'll be marching,
　With bright laurels on my brow,
I have for my country fallen,
　Who will care for mother now?

*Chorus*:  Soon with angels, etc.

# Pray, Maiden, Pray

Words: A. W. Kercheval
Music: A. J. Turner

This ballad was dedicated "For the Times" and "To The Patriotic Women of the South." The girl is to pray for her loved one in battle, and for the cause:

"For Home, for Freedom and the Right,
Pray, Maiden, Pray"

dead - ly\_\_ fight! Pray, maid - en, pray!_____

Pray,_____ maid - en, pray! pray!

2.

Maiden, pray that the banner high
   Advanced, our cross may wave
And foemen's shot and steel defy!
   In triumph floating o'er the brave
   Who strike for freedom or the grave.
      Pray, maiden, pray!

3.

Maiden, pray for thy Southern land
   Of streams and sunlit skies;
See thou her living greatness stand!
   While in her hero-dust there lies
   Whatever glory defies!
      Pray, maiden, pray!

4.

Maiden, pray that yon trumpet blast
   And rocket's signal light
But summon squadrons thick and fast!
   To win in our victorious fight
   For Home for Freedom and the Right.
      Pray, maiden, pray!

# Foes and Friends

Words and Music:
George F. Root

This hymn-like song portrays a soldier from New Hampshire and one from Georgia who in day time were foes and at night, dying on the red clay field, become friends. They both pray for their dear ones at home whom they will see no more.

Moderato

1. Two sol - diers ly -ing as they fell, Up - on the red-dened clay, In day - time foes, at night in peace, Breath'd there their lives a - way; Brave hearts had stirr'd each man-ly breast, Fate, on - ly, made them foes; And

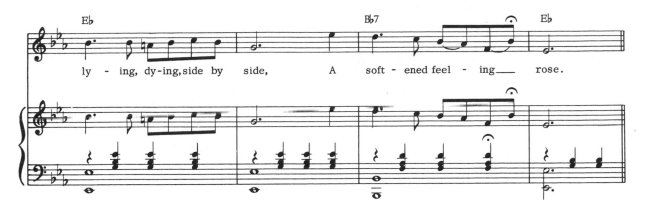

ly - ing, dy-ing, side by side, A soft - ened feel - ing____ rose.

*Chorus*

They'll__ go no more to the lov'd homes here, But to - geth - er both__ will__ wait____ For the

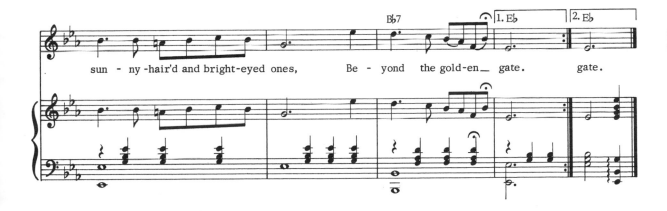

sun - ny - hair'd and bright-eyed ones, Be - yond the gold-en__ gate. gate.

2.

"Among New Hampshire's snowy hills,
  There pray for me tonight
A woman and a little girl,
  With hair like golden light;"
And at the thought, broke forth at last
  The cry of anguish wild,
That would not longer be repressed,
"O God, my wife, my child!"

*Chorus*: They'll go no more, etc.

### 3.
Then spoke the other dying man;
 "Across the Georgia plain,
There watch and wait for me loved ones
 I'll never see again;
A little girl, with dark bright eyes,
 Each day is at the door,
The father's step, the father's kiss
 Will never greet her more."

*Chorus*: They'll go no more, etc.

### 4.
The dying lips the pardon breathe,
 The dying hands entwine;
The last ray dies, and over all
 The stars of heaven shine,
And now, the girl with golden hair,
 And she with dark eyes bright,
On Hampshire's hills and Georgia's plain,
 Were fatherless that night.

*Chorus*: They'll go no more, etc.

# Weeping, Sad and Lonely
### or
### When the Cruel War is Over

Words: Charles Carroll Sawyer
Music: Henry Tucker

It is reported that the sale of this song approached a million copies, and that it was very popular with both the North and the South. So depressing were the sentiments of "Weeping, Sad and Lonely" that officers forbade its singing. The Southern soldiers substituted "grey" for "blue."

Slowly and sadly

When you vow'd to me and coun - try Ev - er to be true.

*Chorus*

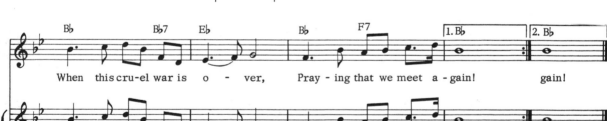

Weep - ing, sad and lone - ly, Hopes and fears how__ vain!

When this cru-el war is o - ver, Pray - ing that we meet a - gain! gain!

2.
When the summer breeze is sighing
Mournfully along,
Or when autumn leaves are falling,
Sadly breathes the song.
Oft in dreams I see thee lying
On the battle plain,
Lonely, wounded, even dying.
Calling, but in vain.

*Chorus*: Weeping, sad, etc.

3.

If amid the din of battle
  Nobly you should fall,
Far away from those who love you,
  None to hear you call —
Who would whisper words of comfort,
  Who would soothe your pain?
Ah! the many cruel fancies
  Ever in my brain.

*Chorus:* Weeping, sad, etc.

4.

But our country called you, darling,
  Angels cheer your way;
While our nation's sons are fighting,
  We can only pray.
Nobly strike for God and liberty,
  Let all nations see
How we love the starry banner,
  Emblem of the free.

*Chorus:* Weeping, sad, etc.

# When upon the Field of Glory
## Answer to
## When the Cruel War Is Over

Words: John Hill Hewitt
Music: H. L. Schreiner

This is the Southern reply to "Weeping, Sad and Lonely." The spirit of heroism and militancy veils the feelings of pessimism.

Moderately, with much expression

1. When up-on the field of glo - ry, 'Mid the bat - tle cry,

And the smoke of can-non curl - ing Round the moun - tain high;

Then sweet mem-'ries will come o'er me, Paint - ing home and thee;

Nerv - ing me to deeds of dar - ing, Strug - gling to be free.

**Chorus**

Weep no long - er, dear - est, Tears are now in vain. _____

When this cru-el war is o - ver, We may meet a - gain. gain.

2.
Oft I think of joys departed,
   Oft I think of thee;
When night's sisters throw around me
   Their star'd canopy.
Dreams so dear come o'er my pillow,
   Bringing up the past.
Oh! how sweet the soldier's visions!
   Oh! how short they last!

*Chorus*: Weep no longer, etc.

### 3.

When I stand, a lonely picket,
    Gazing on the moon,
As she walks her starry pathway,
    In night's silent noon;
I will think that thou art looking
    On her placid face.
Then our tho'ts will meet together
    In a heav'nly place.

*Chorus*:  Weep no longer, etc.

### 4.

When the bullet, swiftly flying
    Thro' the murky air
Hits its mark, my sorrow'd bosom,
    Leaving death's pang there;
Then my tho'ts on thee will turn, love,
    While I prostrate lie.
My pale lips shall breathe "God bless thee —
    For our cause I die!"

*Chorus : After Last Verse)*
    Weep then for me, dearest,
    When I free from pain;
    When this cruel war is over,
    In Heav'n we'll meet again.

THE SOLDIER'S DREAM OF HOME.

# Part Five

# *Memories*

# We Were Comrades Together in the Days of War

Words: Col. Joe Whitfield
Music: Collin Coe

This spirited song recalls the march, the battle and the bugle call to arms. It toasts the dear ones who fell in battle, and sings of meeting them under the star of liberty—for "we are also growing old together since the war."

**Chorus**

Don't you hear the bu-gle call-ing, com-rades, to-day? Echo-ing still in mem-'ry of the days pass'd a-way! Ral-ly round the camp-fire, from near and from far; We were com-rades to-geth-er in the days of the war. days of the war.

2.

We have march'd along together
   In the sun and the rain;
We've fac'd the fight together,
   And together borne the pain!
And each one tells his story
   Of the wound or the scar —
We were comrades together
   In the days of the war.

*Chorus*: Don't you hear, etc.

3.

To the dear ones gone before us,
   Here's a health, comrades all!
We soon shall go to meet them,
   At the last great bugle call!
Beneath the star of Liberty,
   The bright, shining star —
We're growing old together
   Since the days of the war.

*Chorus*: Don't you hear, etc.

# We've Drunk from the Same Canteen

Words: Miles O'Reilly
Music: James G. Clark

With an air of optimism, the soldier recalls the events and friendships made during the long period of strife. The rich can drink their "golden potations" in glasses of crystal and green, but there's nothing like sharing and drinking from the same canteen.

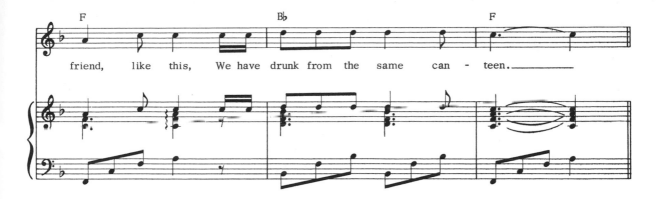

friend, like this, We have drunk from the same can - teen.____

*Chorus*

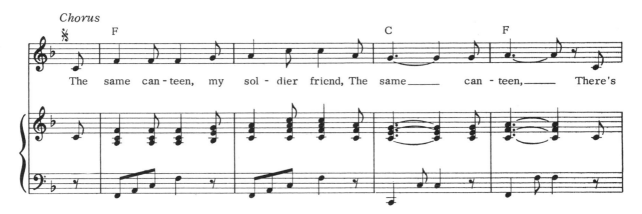

The same can-teen, my sol-dier friend, The same____ can-teen,____ There's

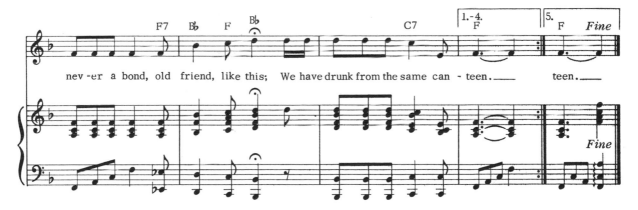

nev-er a bond, old friend, like this; We have drunk from the same can - teen.____ teen.____

*Fine*

5. For when wound - ed I lay on the out - er slope, With my

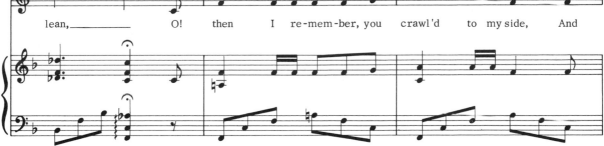

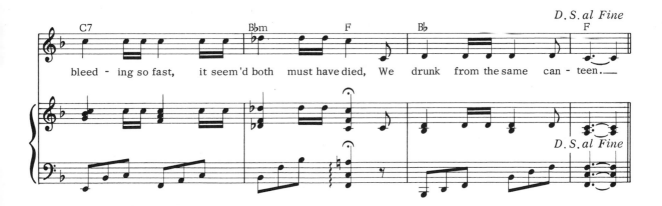

**2.**
It was sometimes water, and sometimes milk,
Sometimes applejack, fine as silk,
But whatever the tipple has been,
We shar'd it together, in bane or bliss,
And I warm to you friend, when I think of this,
We have drunk from the same canteen.

*Chorus*: The same canteen, etc.

3.

The rich and the great sit down to dine,
And quaff to each other in sparkling wine,
From glasses of crystal and green.
But I guess in their golden potations they miss
The warmth of regard, to be found in this;
We have drunk from the same canteen.

*Chorus*: The same canteen, etc.

4.

We've shar'd our blankets and tent together,
And march'd and fought in all kinds of weather,
And hungry and full we've been.
Had days of battle, and days of rest,
But this mem'ry I cling to and love the best,
We have drunk from the same canteen.

*Chorus*: The same canteen, etc.

5.

For when wounded I lay on the outer slope,
With my blood flowing fast, and but little hope,
On which my faint spirit might lean,
O! then I remember, you crawl'd to my side,
And bleeding so fast, it seem'd both must have died,
We drunk from the same canteen.

*Chorus*: The same canteen, etc.

# Brother, Tell Me of the Battle

Words: Thomas Manahan
Music: George F. Root

When a soldier came home, the family and neighbors usually gathered around and eagerly asked for news of the war effort and the "dear ones" in battle. In this song the sister asks her brother about the battle. She had been told that he had fallen, but now that he is back home she wants to know about his heroic deeds and how he fought the foe.

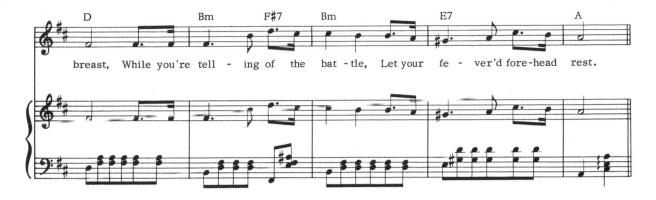

breast, While you're tell - ing of the bat -tle, Let your fe - ver'd fore-head rest.

*Chorus*

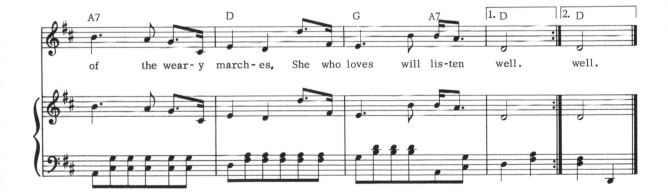

Broth - er, tell me of the bat - tle, How the sol - diers fought and fell,___ Tell me

of the wear-y march - es, She who loves will lis-ten well. well.

### 2.

Brother, tell me of the battle,
    For they said your life was o'er,
They all told me you had fallen,
    That I'd never see you more;
Oh, I've been so sad and lonely,
    Fill'd my breast has been with pain,
Since they said my dearest brother
    I should never see again.

*Chorus*: Brother, tell me, etc.

### 3.

Brother, tell me of the battle,
    I can bear to hear it now,
Lay your head upon my bosom,
    Let me soothe your fever'd brow.
Tell me are you badly wounded?
    Did we win the deadly fight?
Did the vict'ry crown our banner?
    Did you put the foe to flight?

*Chorus*: Brother, tell me, etc.

# Tell Me, Is My Father Coming Home?

Words: W. Dexter Smith, Jr.
Music: Frederick Buckley

The incident upon which this song is based was recorded on its title page:

"As one of our volunteer regiments was passing through one of the principal streets of Boston on its return from the seat of war, a little fellow pushed his way through the crowd assembled, and running up to one of the officers enquired, "Is my father coming home?"

Moderately, with feeling

1. Tell me, is my Fath - er com - ing Home a - gain, to us today? Oh! the days have been so cheer - less, Since he went so far a-
way. I re-mem-ber when he left us, When your reg - i - ment passed

by, And our tears were sad - ly fall - ing, As he bade us all "Good bye."

*Chorus*

Tell me, is my Fath - er com - ing, com - ing, Com - ing home to us to - day?

Oh! the days have been so cheer-less, Since he has been so far a - way. way.

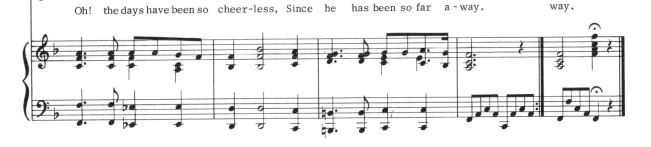

**2.**

Tell me, is my Father coming?
   I am sure he went with you,
And I see familiar faces
   Of the comrades that he knew
All along your ranks I'm looking,
   Yet I cannot see his face.
It may be that he is wounded;
   That a stranger fills his place.

*Chorus*: Tell me, is my Father, etc.

**3.**

Oh! I cannot tell my mother
   Fears that in my sad heart burn,
Do not say that he has fallen
   That he never will return;
For I thought that he was coming
   When I heard the joyful drum.
Soldiers, do not turn your faces,
   Tell me, has my Father come?

*Chorus*: Tell me, is my Father, etc.

# When Johnny Comes Marching Home

Words and Music:
Patrick Sarsfield Gilmore

This song has endured throughout the years. Both Confederate and Union Soldiers used it for parody. At New Orleans the Confederates sang it to the title "For Bales" and at Gettysburg, the Union soldiers sang about the "Boys of the Potomac," about McClellan, Pope, Burnside and Meade. The home folks sang with joy and hope about the day "When Johnny Comes Marching Home."

Pat Gilmore was the band master of the Union Armies.

all feel gay, When John-ny comes march-ing home. home.

2.

The old church bell will peal with joy,
    Hurrah! Hurrah!
To welcome home our darling boy,
    Hurrah! Hurrah!
The village lads and lassies say
With roses they will strew the way,
And we'll all feel gay
    When Johnny comes marching home.

3.

Get ready for the Jubilee,
    Hurrah! Hurrah!
We'll give the hero three times three;
    Hurrah! Hurrah!
And laurel is ready now
To place upon his loyal brow.
And we'll all feel gay
    When Johnny comes marching home.

4.

Let love and friendship on that day,
    Hurrah! Hurrah!
Their choicest treasures then display;
    Hurray! Hurrah!
And let each one perform some part
To fill with joy the warrior's heart,
And we'll all feel gay
    When Johnny comes marching home.

# The Vacant Chair

Words: H. S. Washburn
Music: George F. Root

Written in 1861, about Thanksgiving time, the theme of the "vacant chair" was a familiar one in Northern and Southern homes. The song commemorates the death of Lt. John William Grout, Massachusetts Infantry, who was killed at Ball's Bluff in October, 1861.

Slowly, with feeling

1. We shall meet, but we shall miss him There will be one va-cant chair; We shall lin - ger to ca - ress him While we breathe our ev'n-ing prayer. When one year a - go we gath-ered, Joy was in his mild blue

eye, Now the gold - en cord is sev-ered, And our hopes in ru-in lie.

*Chorus*

We shall meet but we shall miss him, There will be one va-cant chair; We shall

lin - ger to ca-ress him While we breathe our ev'n-ing prayer. 2. At our prayer.

**2.**

At our fireside, sad and lonely,
　Often will the bosom swell
At remembrance of the story
　How our noble Willie fell;
How he strove to bear our banner
　Thro' the thickest of the fight,
And uphold our country's honor
　In the strength of manhood's might.

*Chorus:* We shall meet, etc.

**3.**

True they tell us wreaths of glory
　Evermore will deck his brow,
But this soothes the anguish only
　Sweeping o'er our heartstrings now.
Sleep today O' early fallen
　In thy green and narrow bed,
Dirges from the pine and cypress
　Mingle with the tears we shed.

*Chorus:* We shall meet, etc.

# The Songs We Sang upon the Old Camp Ground

Words and Music:
H. L. Frisbie

War always brings memories—some humorous and some painful. The memory of singing together at camp, on the march and in battle is one which lingers on.

Slowly

1. Oh,___ sing for me to-night those mer - ry songs we sang When bright and warm the cheer-ful camp-fire blaz'd, At___ twi - light's clos - ing hour with com - rades gath - er'd round, We gai - ly sang those oft re - peat - ed

lays. How__ quick - ly beats my heart when comes the ech - oed strain, I

lis - ten then to catch the faint - est sound. I__ nev - er can for - get those

old fa - mil - iar tones: Those songs we sang up - on the old camp ground.

*Chorus*

Yes,__ sing for me to night those brave and mer - ry songs, Let

sweet-er mem-'ries clus-ter thick a - round, For I nev-er can for-get those old fa - mil - iar strains, Those songs we sang up - on the old camp ground. songs we sang up - on the old camp ground.

**2.**

I hear the bugle pealing forth its brazen notes;
I listen to the rolling of the drum;
The sounding call to arms, the battle's clash and din,
Like mocking echoes with the songs they come.
The fire is burning low, the sentry lonely treads
With slow and measur'd step his weary round,
All these I seem to see as I listen to those songs:
Those songs we sang upon the old camp ground.

*Chorus*: Yes, sing for me, etc.

**3.**

Where are my comrades now? ah! why am I alone!
Go ask it of the marching echo, why?
Go stand upon the plain and count their lowly graves,
Where on a hundred battlefields they lie.
Then wonder not that I should love those simple songs,
That sadder mem'ries cluster thick around:
Tho' others may be sweet none are so dear to me
As those we sang upon the old camp ground.

*Chorus*: Yes, sing for me, etc.

# Wearing of the Grey

Words: "O. K. P.
Music: "Wearing of the Green"

The Confederate soldier fought well for the cause as he saw it at the time. Now the war has come to an end, and the soldier nostalgically reminisces about the suit of Grey.

Moderato

1. The___ fear-ful strug-gle's end-ed now, And Peace smiles on our land, And though we've yield-ed, we have proved our-selves a faith-ful band; We___ fought them long, we fought them well, We fought them night and day, And brave-ly strug-gled for our rights, While

wear- ing of the Grey. And___ now that we have ceas'd to fight And

pledged our sa -cred word That___ we a -gainst the Un -ion's might No

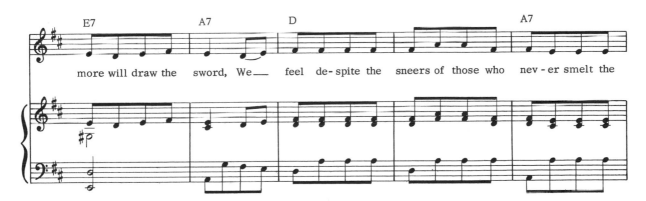

more will draw the sword, We___ feel de -spite the sneers of those who nev -er smelt the

fray, That we've a man -ly, hon -est right To wear -ing of the Grey.

**2.**

Our cause is lost! No more we fight
    'Gainst overwhelming power,
All wearied are our limbs, and drenched
    With many a battle shower.
We fain would rest.  For want of strength
    We yield them up the day,
And lower the flag so proudly borne
    While wearing of the Grey.

**3.**

Defeat is not dishonor.  No!
    Of honor not bereft,
We should thank God that in our breasts
    This priceless boon is left.
And though we weep, 'tis for those braves
    Who stood in proud array
Beneath our flag, and nobly died
    While wearing of the Grey.

**4.**

When in the ranks of war we stood
    And faced the deadly hail,
Our simple suits of grey composed
    Our only coats of mail;
And of those awful hours that marked
    The bloody battle-day
In memory we'll still be seen
    A wearing of the Grey.

**5.**

Oh! should we reach that glorious place
    Where waits the sparkling crown
For every one who for the Right
    His soldier-life lay down;
God grant to us the privilege
    Upon that happy day,
Of clasping hands with those who fell
    A wearing of the Grey.

# Good-bye, Old Glory

Words: L. J. Bates
Music: George F. Root

The Union soldier also fought well for the cause as he saw it at the time. With high hopes for peace, the soldier bids adieu to the fight, the march, the bugle and the hard tack. Now that it's all over, the Union soldier will doff his army Blue.

drums and bu - gles____ loud and fast, This____ is your last tat - too.

*Chorus*

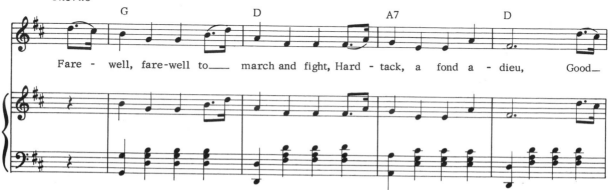

Fare - well, fare-well to____ march and fight, Hard - tack, a fond a - dieu, Good____

bye "Old Glo - ry,"____ for to - night We____ doff the ar - my blue.

2.
O comrades that may ne'er return,
  Who sleep beneath the dew.
Where Vicksburg's gleaming signal's burn
  Or look out's crest of blue.
Where'er your blood has sealed the faith,
  We brought in triumph through.
Goodnight to glory and to death,
  And that's good morn to you.

*Chorus*: Farewell, farewell, etc.

### 3.

Farewell to pens and prison holes,
    Where friends themselves broke through,
And tortured noble captive souls
    That they could not subdue.
But in the fullness of the day
    Heaven's justice did we do.
Disaster, famine, ruin, may
    Make fearful answer true.

*Chorus*: Farewell, farewell, etc.

### 4.

Goodbye to muster and parade,
    Goodbye the grand review.
The dusty line, the dashing aid,
    Goodbye our general too.
Goodbye to war, but halt! I say,
    John Bull a word with you.
Pay up old scores or we again
    May don the army blue.

*Chorus*: Farewell, farewell, etc.

# Selected Bibliography

This list of books is presented in the hope that those who enjoy the music presented in THE SINGING SOLDIERS will go on to more American folk music. Part I of this list presents collections of music; Part II lists sources for the history of the music, and the times which produced it.

PART I

*Allan's Lone Star Ballads,* F. D. Allan, ed., Texas, 1874.

*American Songster,* John Kenedy, Baltimore, 1836.

*American War Songs,* privately printed, Philadelphia, 1925.

*Beadle's Dime Union Song Book,* (3 vols.) Beadle and Company, New York, 1861.

*Bugle Call, The,* G. F. Root, ed., Chicago, 1863.

*Campfire Songster, The,* Albert Davis Collection, 1863.

*Christy's Plantation Melodies,* E. P. Christy, Fisher and Brother, Philadelphia, 1851.

*Grand Army War Songs,* W. G. Smith, ed., S. Brainard & Sons, Cleveland, 1886.

*Harrison's Comic Songster,* W. B. Harrison, Dick and Fitzgerald, New York, c. 1862.

*Hutchinson's Republican Songster,* J. W. Hutchinson, ed., O. Hutchinson, New York, 1860.

*Little Mac Songster, The,* Dick and Fitzgerald, New York, c. 1862.

*Log Cabin and Hard Cider Songster, The,* Boston, 1840.

*Our National War Songs,* S. Brainard's Sons, Chicago, 1892.

*Rebel Rhymes and Rhapsodies,* Frank Moore, ed. G. P. Putnam, New York, 1864.

*Rough and Ready Songster, The,* Nafis and Cornish, New York, c. 1848.

*Songs of Dixie,* S. Brainard's Sons, New York, 1890.

*Songs of Forest and River Folk,* P. Glass and L. Singer, Grosset & Dunlap, New York, 1967.

*Songs of Henry Clay Work,* Collected Edition, Chicago, 1864.

*Songs of Hill and Mountain Folk,* P. Glass and L. Singer, Grosset & Dunlap, New York, 1967.

*Songs of Love and Liberty,* Marinda Branson Moore, Branson and Farrar, Raleigh, North Carolina, 1864.

*Songs of the Confederacy,* R. B. Harwell, Broadcast Music, Inc., New York, 1951.

*Songs of the Sea,* P. Glass and L. Singer, Grosset & Dunlap, New York, 1966.

*Songs of the West,* P. Glass and L. Singer, Grosset & Dunlap, New York, 1966.

*Songs of Town and City Folk*, P. Glass and L. Singer ,Grosset & Dunlap, New York, 1967.
*Sound Off!*, E. A. Dolph, Farrar—Rinehart, New York, 1942.
*Southern Songs of the Confederacy*, Kate Stanton, ed., New York, 1926.
*Tony Pastor's New Union Song Book*, Dick and Fitzgerald, New York, 1862.
*Touch the Elbow Songster*, Dick and Fitzgerald, New York, 1862.
*War Songs for Freemen*, F. J. Child, ed., Ticknor and Fields, Boston, 1863.

PART II
*Ballad of America*, J. A. Scott, Grosset & Dunlap, New York, 1967.
*Battles and Leaders of the Civil War*, R. U. Johnson and C. C. Buel, T. Yoseloff, New York, 1956.
*Belle of the Fifties, A*, Ada Sterling, ed., Doubleday-Page, New York, 1904.
*Blue and the Gray, The*, Henry S. Commager, Bobbs Merrill, New York, 1950.
*Civil War History*, A. T. Luper, ed., University of Iowa, 1958.
*Confederate Music*, R. B. Harwell, University of North Carolina Press, 1950.
*Early American Sheet Music: Its Lure and Its Lore*, H. Dichter and E. Shapiro, R. P. Bowker, New York, 1941.
*History of Popular Music in America*, S. G. Spaeth, Random House, Toronto, 1948.
*Life of Billy Yank, The*, B. I. Wiley, Bobbs Merrill, 1952.
*Life of Johnny Reb, The*, B. I. Wiley, Bobbs Merrill, 1943.
*National Hymns*, Richard White, Budd Carleton, New York, 1886.
*Our American Music*, J. T. Howard, T. Y. Crowell, New York, 1946.
*Pen and Ink*, Brander Matthews, Longmans Green, New York, 1894.
*Personal Portraits*, J. E. Cooke, E. B. Treat, New York, 1872.
*Read 'em and Weep*, S. G. Spaeth, Doubleday, New York, 1927.
*Singing Sixties, The*, W. & P. Heaps, University of Oklahoma Press, 1960.
*Southern Girl in '61, A*, D. Giraud Wright, Doubleday-Page, New York, 1905.
*This Hallowed Ground*, Bruce Catton, Doubleday, New York, 1954.